Leabharlann
Chondae an Chabháin

Batty, Bloomers and Boycott

A little etymology of
eponymous words

Rosie Boycott

Hutchinson
London Melbourne Sydney Auckland Johannesburg

Hutchinson & Co. (Publishers) Ltd

An imprint of the Hutchinson Publishing Group

17–21 Conway Street, London W1P 6JD

Hutchinson Group (Australia) Pty Ltd
30–32 Cremorne Street, Richmond South, Victoria 3121
PO Box 151, Broadway, New South Wales 2007

Hutchinson Group (NZ) Ltd
32–34 View Road, PO Box 40-086, Glenfield, Auckland 10

Hutchinson Group (SA) Pty Ltd
PO Box 337, Bergvlei 2012, South Africa

First published 1982
© Rosie Boycott 1982

Set in VIP Baskerville by
D.P. Media Limited, Hitchin, Hertfordshire

Printed in Great Britain by The Anchor Press Ltd
and bound by Wm Brendon & Son Ltd,
both of Tiptree, Essex

British Library Cataloguing in Publication Data

Boycott, Rosie
  Batty, bloomers and boycott: a little etymology
  of eponymous words
  1. English language–Eponyms–Vocabularies,
  glossaries, etc.
  I. Title
  423   PE1596

ISBN 0 09 149850 3

To my father

Acknowledgements

I should like to thank the following people for their invaluable help in the research and compilation of this book: Major Charles Boycott, for contributing the entry about Captain Boycott; Mrs Betty Easton, for permission to use material from the unpublished book written by her late father H. A. C. Goodwin MA; Nigel Viney, for his careful and painstaking reading of the manuscript; Vanessa Armstrong, for typing it; Robert and Elizabeth Willis, for the enormous number of eponyms they produced; Karen Durbin of *Village Voice*, for having me to stay while I researched in the New York Public Library; Christopher Logue, who generously allowed me to read his research for a similar project; and a special thank-you to my editor, Susan Hill.

Introduction

An eponymous word is one that has entered the English language because of a person or that person's deeds. The word derives from the name. When I first began to research this book, I thought that there might be perhaps sixty words in the language that fitted my original, rather rigid definition. I wanted to include only those words that had become so much part of the language that they functioned not just as proper nouns, but as verbs, common nouns or adjectives as well. Only those words which had lost their obvious personal associations along with their capital letter, I thought. My own name, Boycott, which is one of the better-known eponyms, fulfils such demands. So, indeed, do many other words, such as *gerrymander* or *galvanize*.

Research unearthed far more words than I had anticipated. Many of these did not fit the original definition, but were, nevertheless, in common currency, or were words which I thought worthy of inclusion either because of their surprising origins (often at odds with what might have been seen to be an obvious, non-eponymous derivation), or because of the story lying behind their place in the language. For instance, I had always thought that the expression *your name is mud* stemmed from an allusion to messy, thick, wet matter. It would make sense. The phrase's origins are, in fact, much more bizarre.

Another early decision was to exclude words from fiction or mythology, such as *Scrooge* or *aphrodisiac*. But this criterion for selection would have excluded several interestingly derived words which are in common usage – *diddle*, *panic*, etc. – so I have mentioned some of the lesser-known literary and mythological eponyms.

Although words have been coined eponymously since the beginnings of language, the largest number of eponyms date from the Industrial Revolution. The sudden influx into everyday life of scientific concepts, discoveries and inventions produced a need for new words. These frequently were derived from the brains behind the idea or object to be named. Words such as *volt*, *ohm*, *amp*, *geiger-counter* and *diesel* were derived in this way. I have chosen to include here only those scientific words which are in relatively common usage, for the terminology of science is frequently eponymous. The human body alone has over a hundred parts which are named after their identifiers, and numerous diseases take their names from the doctor who isolated the particular virus or malfunction. Terms from botany, physics and the culinary arts are also largely eponymously derived, so I have been selective.

Places, streets and countries are often named after people. Sloane Street receives a mention. It was named, as were Sloane Square, Sloane Avenue and Hans Crescent, after Sir Hans Sloane. In recent years that area of London has become associated with a prototype figure – the Sloane Ranger. But where a town or country has been named in honour of an individual – such as Washington – it has usually been excluded, since the word has no other linguistic function.

Certain institutions have been included since their names have become synonymous with particular styles. The Ritz Hotel is the source of several words, chiefly the adjective *ritzy* and the phrase *putting on the Ritz*. Young César Ritz, the thirteenth child of a Swiss peasant, may have been surprised. Other people, like William Burke and Mr Bishop, enriched the language, ironically, through infamous deeds.

As society and life change, so do words. The need

for new ones arises when a certain action or mannerism becomes so widely understood or used that it is no longer sufficient or indeed necessary to describe it in long analogies. The term to *boycott* is one example. Boycotting was a political practice for centuries, but it was only when the plight of Captain Boycott attracted international attention that it became necessary to find a single word to describe the process of social ostracism as a political tool.

Many of the words in the book have disputed origins; frequently the stories behind certain eponymous words have become part of modern mythology; and some of the tales are possibly apocryphal. Inevitably, the discerning reader will find gaps, or may be puzzled by some of my choices for inclusion. In the end, any book which does not claim to be a definitive dictionary is wholly made up of the author's selections.

Abigail

An *Abigail* is a little-used name for a handmaiden or lady's maid.

In the Book of Samuel, Abigail, the wife of Nabal, is described as a woman of 'good understanding, and of a beautiful countenance', though her husband was 'churlish and evil in his doings'. She was intelligent, and employed her cunning and strategy to prevent David from taking his bloody revenge on her husband and his men. When Nabal died ten days later, Abigail, who was never slow to seize an opportunity, married David without delay. She proclaimed herself his handmaiden, 'a servant to wash the feet of the servants of my lord'.

The name came into general use in Beaumont and Fletcher's play *The Scornful Lady* (1610), in which the 'waiting gentlewoman' is named Abigail after the biblical character.

Adam's apple

Adam's apple is the common name for the projection of the thyroid cartilage of the larynx.

Tradition has it that the name derives from the belief that a piece of apple from the forbidden tree, given to Adam by Eve, stuck in his throat. Where this story came from is a mystery, since there is no reference to it in the Bible. In Genesis 3:3, God says of the tree, 'Ye shall not eat of it, neither shall ye touch it, lest ye die.' As everyone knows, the instruction was disregarded.

Adam's ale is a euphemism for water: the first human obviously had nothing else with which to quench his thirst.

Albert

An *Albert* is a watch chain which stretches across a waistcoat from one pocket to the other, and is so called in honour of Prince Albert (1819–61), who originally set the fashion. In 1849 when he was visiting Birmingham, he was presented with such a chain by the jewellers of the town. He was pleased with his gift and wore it from then on.

America

The continent of America should, perhaps, have been called Columbus, after its true discoverer the explorer Christopher Columbus. That it was named America came about as a result of a series of fabricated letters and accounts.

Amerigo Vespucci (1451–1512) was a merchant, born in Florence, who worked for the company run by Gianotto Berardi, who fitted out ships for, amongst others, Christopher Columbus. However, in 1499 Vespucci made his own voyage of discovery, to Venezuela, and then returned to live in Spain where he became, from 1508, the pilot-major of the kingdom. In 1507, in St Die in Lorraine, an inaccurate account of his travels was published, in which it was claimed that he had reached the mainland of America in 1497. (Columbus had reached the South American mainland for the first time in 1498.) The two continents were duly named in Amerigo's honour. Sir Clements Markham, the nineteenth-century English geographer, translated Vespucci's letters in 1894 and proved that at least one of them was a total fabrication and that the others were quite unsupported by concrete evidence.

Ampere

The *ampere* is the definitive unit of electrical current; precisely, 1 amp is the unit of current that 1 volt can send through 1 ohm.

André Marie Ampère (1775–1836), the French mathematician and physicist who was born at Polemieux near Lyons, eventually became professor of mathematics at the Ecole Polytechnique, a member of the Academie des Sciences and a foreign member of the Royal Society. He was the first scientist to explain that the earth's magnetism is a result of terrestrial electrical currents circulating from east to west.

Although his career was marked by brilliance and hard work, his private life was deeply unhappy. When he was only eighteen his father was executed in the Reign of Terror. The shock was so great that the young André did not speak for over a year. Eventually he resumed his studies, taking intensive courses in algebra. He married when he was twenty-four, but his wife died shortly afterwards. Ampère was once again plunged into deep gloom, but found solace in his work.

Atlas

A book of maps or a size of paper.

In Greek mythology, Atlas was one of the Titans who, because of his part in their attempt to overthrow Zeus, was condemned to spend the rest of his life supporting the pillars of heaven on his shoulders. His name was given to the Atlas mountains of Africa where, according to legend, Atlas went to perform his task as they were the closest to the heavens.

According to some accounts, Atlas was relieved of his burden when Heracles offered to support the heavens if Atlas would pick the apples of Hesperides for him. Atlas loved his new freedom and offered to take them back home for him, but Heracles was not to be outsmarted. He persuaded Atlas to hold the heavens for a moment while he found a cushion for his back, and then departed with the apples, leaving the Titan with his burden.

A book of maps is called an *atlas* because Mercator, an early map-maker, put a figure of Atlas supporting the world on his shoulders on the title page of his first collection of maps, published in 1595. (Similar collections had been published previously.)

In the paper trade, *atlas* is the name given to a standard size of drawing paper measuring 34 by 26 inches.

August

The eighth month of the year and the adjective describing impressive and dignified behaviour both derive from the first Roman emperor Augustus Caesar (63 BC–AD 14). Prior to Julius Caesar, Augustus's great-uncle, the Roman calendar had only consisted of ten months (March to December), as the year was reckoned as 304 days. However, with the introduction of the solar year, January and February were added to make up the remaining days. Caesar decided to rename one of the old months, formerly called Quintilis because it used to be the fifth, after himself – hence July. Not to be outdone, Augustus decided to do the same some years later and considered which month to

choose. In the end he decided on the old month of Sextilis
(the sixth), because it had always been lucky for him. In
Sextilis he had begun his first consulship, celebrated three
triumphs, obtained the allegiance of the legions of
Janiculum and ended the civil wars. Thus in 8 BC the name
of the month was changed to Augustus.

Bacchanalian

The modern adjective to describe a drunken orgy on a
grand scale derives from the Roman god, Bacchus. As the
god of wine, he symbolized the fruitfulness and blessing of
autumn. The festivals held in Rome to celebrate the harvest
and also Bacchus's wedding to Ariadne were characterized
by their drunkenness. At first the *bacchanalia* were held in
secret three times a year and were open only to women, but
men were later admitted. The festivals eventually became
so licentious that they were banned.

Baedeker

These authoritative travel guides were first published in
Germany by Karl Baedeker.

Baedeker was born in 1801, in Essen, the son of a printer
and bookseller. He set up a similar business in Koblenz and
achieved immediate success with the publication of his first
guide, *A Rhineland Journey from Basle to Düsseldorf*. Many
other guides followed, covering various parts of Europe and
published in various languages. Baedeker's success
depended on his ability to assess different regions in an
authoritative and informative way, always recommending
places of interest and providing useful historical and
geographical information, thus eliminating the need for
paid guides. When he died in 1859, most of Europe had
been covered by his books and *Baedeker* had become a
household name.

During the Second World War the Luftwaffe called the
bombing raids over England in 1941–42 *Baedeker raids*
because with the help of a baedeker they deliberately
selected as targets places of great historical and cultural
importance by way of reprisal for British raids on Cologne

and Lübeck. Attacks on Canterbury, Bath and Norwich resulted from German perusal of the guidebook.

Bakelite

Bakelite is the plastic or synthetic resin which is formed by the condensation of phenols and formaldehyde. Although household goods and ornaments can be fashioned from it, its main use today is in electrical insulation. The name derives from the discoverer of the substance, Leo Hendrik Baekeland (1863–1944), formerly professor of chemistry at Ghent University, who emigrated to the USA in 1889 and became honorary professor of chemical engineering at Columbia University. First discovered in 1905, bakelite was first used commercially *c*. 1907.

Banting

William Banting, a London coffin- and cabinet-maker, was the pioneer of a now popular method of dieting: living on high amounts of protein for short periods and avoiding all fats, starch and sugar.

Banting (1797–1878) published a little book in 1863 entitled *Letter on Corpulence*. Grossly overweight himself (he should have weighed about 142 pounds, but in fact weighed 202 pounds), Banting claimed that his weight was not the result of overindulgence, but despaired that, even so, 'I could not stoop to tie my shoe, nor attend to the little offices humanity requires without considerable pain and difficulty.' He was even forced to walk backwards downstairs to ease the pain in his plump knee joints. On seeking medical advice he was told to diet: several ounces of meat for breakfast, tea without milk or sugar, no bread, no biscuits. Dinner was 5 or 6 ounces of any meat or fish, except salmon or pork, and any vegetables except potatoes or beans. A little wine was permitted, though port, beer and champagne were barred. He was also allowed small amounts of food at tea and supper. On this diet Banting lost 46 pounds in a year (he was sixty-six years old at the time) and lived to a ripe old age. The success of his book meant that before he died he heard his name connected with a new slimming regime – *banting*, the high-protein, low-carbohydrate diet.

Barmy

An adjective meaning stupid or feeble-minded. A number of derivations have been suggested for this word. One is that it is a corruption of Bartholomew, from St Bartholomew who was flayed alive. He can be seen looking rather pathetic holding his skin in his hands in paintings by Michelangelo. As St Bartholomew is patron saint of the feeble-minded, there may be some truth in this suggestion, but another derivation gives *barmy* as a variant of *barm*, the froth on the top of a glass of beer. A third possible explanation is that there was apparently an asylum for the insane in Barming near Maidstone in Kent at one time, and the word derives from this.

Baroque

An artistic style popular in the middle of the seventeenth century, typified by elaborate scrolls and symmetrical ornamentation. Though the *Oxford English Dictionary* says the style was originally applied to the architecture of Francesco Borromini (1599–1667), its chief exponent, many sources derive the word from Federigo Barocci (1535–1612), an Italian artist. Another possible explanation is that it comes from *barocco*, a Portuguese term used in jewellery to describe an irregularly shaped pearl, or from the same word used by Italian Renaissance philosophers for extravagant and far-fetched arguments in Scholastic syllogisms.

Batty

An affectionate euphemism to describe someone who is harmlessly insane. The word derives from Fitzherbert Batty, an eccentric barrister who lived in Spanish Town, Jamaica. In 1839 he was certified as insane, which attracted considerable interest in the London press and resulted in the expression we know today.

Béchamel sauce

Béchamel sauce is a fine white sauce sometimes thickened with cream. The basis for many dishes, béchamel is made from flour, butter and milk, and was named after the steward of Louis XIV, Louis de Béchamel (d. 1703), who is supposed to have invented it.

Belcher

A spotted handkerchief. Jim Belcher (1781–1811) was a prizefighter from Bristol. His trademark was always to wear a handkerchief – usually blue with white spots with dark blue centres – around his neck when he went into the ring. Any handkerchiefs fitting this description became known as *belchers*.

Belisha beacon

Belisha beacons, the illuminated amber globes on black and white banded poles at British pedestrian street crossings, were introduced by Sir Leslie Hore-Belisha (1893–1957) as a road-safety measure. Hore-Belisha was Minister of Transport from 1934 to 1937, and his innovation, as well as gaining him immortality in Britain, proved to be successful in reducing the number of road accidents.

Big Ben

Sir Benjamin Hall (1802–67) was the Chief Commissioner of Works from 1855 to 1858. It was during his time in office that the great hour bell for the clock tower of the Houses of Parliament was cast. However, the original bell of 1856 cracked and was replaced in 1858, its successor being first used the following year. At first the bell was to be called St Stephen's, but the press dubbed it *Big Ben* in honour of Sir Benjamin. The name caught on immediately and has since been applied to the entire clock, quarter bells and all.

Big Ben is London's most famous clock. It has appeared in numerous films as a standard reference point to remind the viewer that he is 'in London', and was first broadcast on the radio on New Year's Eve, 1923. Several years ago it was the direct cause of a death: the coat of a workman who was cleaning the clock became entangled in the mechanism; the man was literally wound into a slow and horrendous death. The ear-shattering noise produced by the clock's mechanism and the bell itself prevented his cries for help from being heard.

Big Bertha

Several German weapons were known as *Big Berthas* during the First World War. Initially the name was applied by the French to the large howitzers used to bombard Liège and Namur in 1914, but later it was used to refer to the 142-ton cannon which shelled Paris in 1918 from a distance of 76 miles.

Soldiers had noticed the resemblance between the guns and the short, stocky build of the owner of the great Krupp armament empire, Bertha Krupp von Bohlen und Halbach (1866–1957). Her father, Friedrich Alfred Krupp, had committed suicide in 1902, and Bertha had inherited the Krupp fortunes. She survived both world wars and died peacefully in Germany. (The cannon itself was not actually made by Krupp, but by Skoda.)

Billio

To do something *like billio* is to do it with great verve and energy. The expression comes from a Puritan divine, Joseph Billio, who founded the Independent Congregation in 1682 at Maldon, Essex. Little is known of him, but his name has survived as a monument to the zeal with which he presumably carried out his life's calling.

Billycock

Billycock is the original name for the round-crowned, narrow-brimmed hat more generally known as the bowler. Prior to Mr Bowler's success with the manufacture of the city gentlemen's uniform hat, Lock's of St James's was producing a low-crowned hat in a similar style. It is said that Lock first produced such a hat in 1850 to satisfy the specifications of a Mr William Coke, a sportsman from Holkham, Norfolk, who thought that the style would be more practical on the sports field than the traditional topper which kept falling off. In the hat trade today, the bowler is still often referred to as a *coke*.

Biro

This word for a ballpoint pen derives from the pen's inventor, László Biró.

Biró was born in Hungary and invented the pen there in

1938. With the rise of Nazism he emigrated to South America to continue his research, and took out a patent in Argentina in 1943. At the end of the Second World War he made contact with an English company who agreed to sponsor and manufacture the pen, but before production started, the company was taken over by the French firm Bic, headed by Baron Biche. Thus in France the ballpoint pen is known as a *bic*, and in England as a *biro*.

When first introduced the pen was extremely popular with the RAF as it wrote better than the fountain pen at high altitudes.

Birrellism

To birrell is to comment on life gently and allusively, spicing good nature with irony, and derives from Augustine Birrell (1850–1933), a British politician and author who began his career as a lawyer. Birrell became Liberal MP for West Fife and later for North Bristol; as Minister for Education he introduced the education bill of 1907 which led to his resignation. After serving as Chief Secretary for Ireland (1907–16), he retired in 1918. He was a shrewd man of great wit, best remembered for his series of witty and urbane essays entitled *Obiter Dicta*.

Bishop

The word *bishop* has two somewhat obscure meanings as well as its ecclesiastical one.

To bishop is to file down the teeth of a horse, thereby obscuring his true age, in the hope of achieving a higher sale price. This crafty idea was first practised by a Mr Bishop, about whom little else is known.

The word also means to kill by drowning. Again, little is known of the Bishop who lent his name to this form of murder except that, in the tradition of Burke and Hare, he drowned a boy in Bethnal Green, London, and sold the body to anatomists.

Black Maria

Black Maria is the slang name given to the black van used by the police to transport prisoners and suspects. The name originated from Maria Lee, a powerfully built American

Negress who kept a lodging house in Boston in the
nineteenth century and often assisted the police in
removing drunk and disorderly customers.

Blanket

A large sheet of soft woollen cloth usually used as a bed
covering. According to some sources the first blankets
ever produced in England were spun on the loom of
Thomas Blanket, a weaver who set up shop in Bristol,
c. 1340.

Blimp

This word, describing a type of observation balloon and, by
association, a person who is dull, slow-witted or a
'windbag', has obscure origins.

Most sources say that the non-rigid airship first used in
1915 for observation purposes and later as a barrage device
owes its name to Horace Short, who coined the word either
from *bloody* plus *limp* or (type) *B* plus *limp*. The cartoonist
David Low made metaphorical and hilarious use of the
image in a character drawn for the London *Evening Standard*
in 1940, and the name Colonel Blimp soon entered the
language. By direct analogy with the airship, Blimp is 'full
of hot air, lacking in backbone and deficient in motive
power', and is depicted as an elderly, unprogressive and
rather reactionary gentleman of somewhat limited
intelligence.

Blimpish and *blimpishness* characterize the behaviour of a
particular kind of English bureaucratic dullard.

Bloomers

Now a slightly wry generic term for loose trousers worn by
women, *bloomers* originally referred to an entire costume
consisting of a jacket, skirt and Turkish-style trousers. The
trousers later became known as bloomers in their own right.

The original ensemble was first introduced into
American society by Mrs Amelia Jenks Bloomer
(1818–94) after an idea by Elizabeth Smith Miller. Mrs
Bloomer was the founder and editor in 1849 of a New York
ladies' journal called *The Lily* which supported the

Temperance Movement. *The Lily* was the first magazine in America edited entirely by a woman; indeed, Mrs Bloomer personally wrote almost all the copy, typed the text and supervised the business and distribution.

For a woman to edit a magazine in those days was a courageous venture, so it was not surprising that Mrs Bloomer eagerly embraced the cause of the newly formed US Women's Rights Movement. She decided that her periodical should espouse the cause of women's dress reform and so she held a ball in July 1851 where she first sported the revolutionary new garment. All women attending, she insisted, could wear what they wished above the waist but below 'we would have a skirt reaching down to nearly halfway between the knee and the ankle, and not made quite so full as is the present fashion. Underneath the skirt, trousers moderately full, in fair mild weather, coming down to the ankle (not instep) and there gathered in by an elastic band. . . . For winter, or wet weather, the trousers also full, but coming down into a boot, which should rise some three or four inches at least above the ankle.'

The fashion found favour in some circles and was considered to be in keeping with current standards of decency. However, it was also greatly ridiculed and became a symbol of radicalism. One clergyman forbade Bloomer girls to enter his church; another, Dr DeWitte Talmage, cited Moses when speaking against Mrs Bloomer's outfits: 'A woman shall not wear anything that pertains to a man' (Deut. 22:5). Mrs Bloomer, with a spirited turn of wit, retorted that that rule was rubbish since there was no difference in the fig leaves worn by Adam and Eve.

Bobby

This affectionate and colloquial name for the British policeman derives from Sir Robert Peel, the great British statesman who was born in Lancashire in 1788. He was educated at Harrow (where he was a classmate of Byron) and at Oxford. In 1812 Peel was appointed Chief Secretary for Ireland and proved himself to be a masterly administrator during troubled times. After two years in the post he instigated the Irish (later Royal Irish) Constabulary, who were nicknamed *peelers*. Later, when as

Home Secretary he passed the Metropolitan Police Act in 1829, the word *bobby* was coined as a slang epithet for the members of the new London police force and subsequently for all British policemen.

Peel died in 1850 from injuries resulting from a fall from his horse while riding down Constitution Hill in London.

Bob's your uncle

This expression, which nowadays implies that something is easy to achieve, has its origins in a situation that was characterized by nepotism rather than by genuine simplicity.

The phrase became popular in the late nineteenth century and is associated with the appointment in November 1887 of Arthur Balfour as Chief Secretary for Ireland by his uncle, the then Prime Minister, Robert Cecil, Lord Salisbury (1830–1903). The appointment of the dilettante man of fashion to such an important post created a furore at the time, but for young Balfour things worked out very well in the end. The phrase stems from a longer saying then current: 'You go and ask for the job – and he remembers your name – and Bob's your uncle.'

Bogart

To bogart a joint means to smoke a marijuana cigarette for longer than etiquette dictates instead of passing it on to the next person.

The American film actor, Humphrey Bogart (1899–1957), lent his name to this modern expression that has grown out of the drug culture. Although in his films Bogart is not to be seen attending hash-smoking parties and *bogarting* joints, he usually smoked cigarettes. In his most famous films, such as *The Maltese Falcon* (1942) where he plays a shoestring detective, a cigarette is seldom out of his mouth. In *To Have and Have Not* (1945), the film version of Ernest Hemingway's novel, the subject of cigarettes comes into the script.

There is a curious English forerunner to the expression that had to do with alcohol, not marijuana. A certain Dr Wright of Colchester, who lived in the nineteenth century, was well known for his tremendous greed for port. At dinner parties he was often to be observed keeping the port, instead of passing it to the guest on his left as custom demands; he would help himself to several glasses before condescending to hand the decanter to his neighbour. *To wright* the port became a popular term among the port-drinking circles of English society.

Booze

Though this slang word for alcohol of any description probably comes from the Middle English *bouse* or *bowse*, meaning to drink, there are some grounds to support the story that it derives from one Colonel E. Booze who, at the beginning of the nineteenth century, produced a popular brand of whisky in bottles shaped like log cabins.

Bosey (or Bosie)

This Australian term for a deceptive way of delivering a cricket ball has a meaning similar to the English word *googly* – a ball which spins and bounces in the opposite direction to that which the batsman expects; specifically, an off-break bowled to a right-handed batsman with what appears to be a leg-break action. It was named after its first practitioner, B. J. T. Bosanquet (1877–1936), who toured Australia with the English side from 1903 to 1904.

During the Second World War the word was used by the RAF to describe a single bomb dropped from a plane.

Bourbon

American whisky. The family name of the royal family of France (with branches in Spain and Italy) from 1589 to 1793 and from 1814 to 1830 derives from the seigneury of Bourbon, in Bourbonnais in central France. On their restoration after the French Revolution, the Bourbons, it was said, had learned nothing and forgotten nothing. Hence in America the name *Bourbon* was applied to the Democratic Party leaders of the southern states, with the implication that they were outmoded and guided by an outlook predating the Civil War.

It was near Georgetown, then in Bourbon County, Kentucky, that in 1789 the Baptist clergyman Elijan Craig

first produced a bottle of the famous whisky made from a
blend of corn, with malt or rye sometimes being added.

Bowdlerize

To expurgate a book by omitting words or passages
regarded as indecent.

Dr Thomas Bowdler was born in 1754 near Bath. He
read medicine at Edinburgh University and worked as a
doctor for some years in London. In 1800 he moved to the
Isle of Wight where he professed to enjoy 'the seclusion'. In
1818 he published his censored, ten-volume edition of
Shakespeare's plays, entitled *The Family Shakespeare*. He
claimed that nothing was added to the text but that he had
omitted 'those words and expressions . . . which cannot
with propriety be read aloud in front of the family'. In *The
Family Shakespeare*, Rosalind and Celia become polite,
Falstaff is never bawdy, and the famous line 'Out damn'd
spot!' becomes 'Out crimson spot!'

Encouraged by the moderate success of this first attempt
to clean up English literature, Bowdler went on to publish
his expurgated version of Gibbon's *History of the Decline and
Fall of the Roman Empire* (1825). Not everyone was
appreciative of his efforts. Many saw as ridiculous his
censorship of Shakespeare (though Swinburne in *Studies in
Prose and Poetry* was later to praise his efforts), and the term
bowdlerize was coined in 1836 to describe any form of
censorship for the sake of apparent moral purity.

In his own defence, Bowdler wrote, 'And shall I be
classed with the assassins of Caesar, because I have
rendered these valuable plays fit for the perusal of our
virtuous females?' He died in 1825.

Bowie knife

A 9–18 inch hunting knife, balanced for throwing and
curved and double-edged at the tip, the *bowie knife* was
named after Colonel Jim Bowie (1796–1836), the hero of the
battle of the Alamo. It was Bowie who popularized the
cutting blade, but he was not its inventor. According to
most sources, the knife was in fact designed by his brother,
Rezin Bowie (1793–1841), who drew an original diagram
and then instructed the blacksmith to forge the knife for him

out of a large metal file. The knife went into action soon afterwards in 1827, when brother Jim used it to his advantage in a duel.

Boycott

Charles Cunningham Boycott (1832–97) was the son of a Protestant clergyman and a member of an established East Anglian family. The event which in 1880 was to fling Boycott from obscurity into a short and perilous notoriety, and from thence into his curious immortality in the dictionaries of the world, was no more than a flutter in the long Irish history of land reform.

Landlords (and their agents) were much hated by the peasants, and frequently accused of exploitation and harsh evictions for nonpayment of rent. In 1879 Michael Davitt formed the Land League, centred in County Mayo, to protect peasant interests. In September 1880 Charles Parnell, then its president, spoke to a large open-air Land League meeting. 'Land-grabbers' – those who took a farm from another who had been evicted for nonpayment of rent – were also hated. To a roar that such men should be shot, Parnell enunciated a more Christian way of dealing with such a person: 'You must shun him on the roadside . . . in the streets . . . in the shop . . . in the fair green and market place and even in the place of worship. By leaving him severely alone . . . by isolating him . . . as if he was a leper of old, you must show him your detestation of the crime he has committed.'

By 1880, Boycott, a retired army captain, had farmed for twenty-seven years, the last seven at Lough Mask House, near Ballinrobe, County Mayo. He acted as agent to Lord Erne for some 1500 acres (on which lived thirty-eight tenant farmers), and he also farmed other land on his own account. He was thus both agent *and* master.

Boycott was then aged forty-eight. He was quiet, determined and obstinate. There is evidence that he farmed well and that he invested to improve his own land. However, two bad potato harvests had followed each other in 1879 and 1880, and Boycott had trouble with three of Lord Erne's tenants who demanded rent reductions which were, in his opinion, unjustified. The Land League saw this as oppression of the poor, and throughout October and November he suffered in a 'deliberate, merciless and scientific way' a *boycott*. As he wrote to *The Times*, his servants were intimidated out of his service, his crops carried away, his stock driven out and the local shopkeepers refused to supply his household. He was fired upon three times and he received threatening letters.

Boycott and his plight, with his crop rotting in the ground, became headline news. A Dublin newspaper proposed a 'relief expedition' to get in his harvest, and this found enthusiastic support in Ulster. In the event some sixty-five men funded by public subscription went to Boycott's relief and collected the harvest, protected by an armed guard. However, Boycott was eventually hounded out of the country and the tenants won their case.

In 1881, with the passing of Gladstone's Land Act, fair rent tribunals were set up, thus greatly improving the situation. Boycott returned to Ireland for a short period but eventually settled in Suffolk in 1886.

Boycott's neologist is almost certainly Father John O'Malley of The Neale, a small parish close to Lough Mask House, and a fervent supporter of the Land League. The story goes that James Redpath, a prominent American journalist, was dining with O'Malley when he said, 'I'm bothered about a word. When people ostracize a land-grabber we call it social excommunication, but we ought to have a different word for a landlord or agent like Boycott . . . ostracism won't do. The peasantry won't understand.' O'Malley agreed, and thought for a moment. 'How would it do to call it to boycott him?'

Braille

Louis Braille evolved the reading system for blind people which is now universally accepted. It consists of six embossed points in an oblong of which the horizontal line can contain two and the vertical three points. There are sixty-three possible combinations, incorporating not only the full alphabet but also numerals, capitals and punctuation.

Braille was born in Coupvray, France, in 1809. His father

was a saddler and the child would spend his time helping cut the leather. At the age of three he accidentally drove an awl into his left eye; the accident resulted in total and permanent blindness in both eyes.

Despite the social reforms instituted by Napoleon, the future for a handicapped child in those days was grim. His father refused to let Louis suffer more than was necessary and enrolled him in an ordinary school, where he proved an apt pupil. He later went on to study at the National Institute for the Blind in Paris.

When ten-year-old Louis arrived, the Institute possessed three books, each in twenty parts weighing 20 pounds. The text was written in large embossed letters to be felt by hand. In this cumbersome manner Louis learned to read; he also showed a remarkable aptitude for playing the piano and organ.

While Braille was studying in Paris, an artillery captain, Charles Barbier, reported his invention of 'night writing'. Dots and dashes in relief on thin card were proving valuable for writing down messages to be communicated during darkness. Barbier brought his work to the Institute and Braille set about improving and refining the technique. In 1829 Braille published his first book in the new system and soon adapted the technique to include musical notation. Having accepted a teaching post at the Institute in 1827, he continued to instruct blind children until his death in 1852. The Braille system was officially adopted by the Insitute in 1844.

Brodie, to do a

To do a brodie is an American expression meaning to faint, die or take a chance. It refers to Steve Brodie, a newsboy who allegedly, in 1886, jumped off the old Brooklyn Bridge into New York's East River for a bet of $200 – and survived. Whether or not the splash was caused by Brodie, his life improved immensely after the event and the attention he received emboldened him to open a bar in the Bowery. In the 1933 classic gangster film *The Bowery*, Brodie was portrayed by the late George Raft.

Brougham

A *brougham* is a closed, usually four-wheeled, one-horse carriage. It was built for and named after Lord Henry Brougham (1778–1868), a prominent Scottish Whig politician and reformer and at one time Lord Chancellor. Designed originally as a gentleman's carriage in 1838, the brougham soon went into public service and was the most popular means of transport in London until eclipsed by the hansom cab.

Buckley's chance

This Australian phrase refers to the remotest of chances.

William Buckley was a convict who escaped in 1803 and managed, against what appeared to be impossible odds, to survive amongst the Aborigines for thirty years, eventually dying in 1856.

Another possible origin of the phrase comes from the name of a Melbourne company called Buckley and Nunn, hence the expression: 'There are just two chances, Buckley's or none.'

Bunsen burner

The *bunsen burner* is used in chemistry laboratories and consists of a metal tube with an adjustable air valve for burning a mixture of coal gas and air giving a smokeless flame of great heat ($c.$ 1850° C). The burner was invented in 1855 by Robert Wilhelm Bunsen (1811–99), a German chemist who lost an eye in a laboratory explosion. Though generally credited to Bunsen, who was a professor at Heidelberg University from 1852 and was involved in the discovery of caesium and rubidium, similar designs had been developed earlier by Desdga and Faraday.

Burke

To burke is to murder by suffocation and hence to suppress or hush something up. The origin of the word lies in a gruesome series of murders.

Discoveries in the science of anatomy at the beginning of the nineteenth century necessitated the supply of large numbers of corpses to medical schools for students and doctors to dissect. Doctors were free to advertise that they would buy corpses from relatives, in 'the cause of medical science'.

William Burke, an Irish navvy born in 1792, emigrated to Scotland *c.* 1818 to dig the Union Canal. In 1827 he took lodgings in the house of a fellow countryman William Hare and his wife in Edinburgh. One day an elderly man died in the boarding house and, as he had no relatives, Burke and Hare took the body to Dr Robert Knox, an Edinburgh anatomist, who offered them cash (£7 10s). This was a substantial amount in those days and Burke and Hare realized they had a potentially profitable trade. Edinburgh was full of lonely old people whom no one would miss. Abigail Simpson, an old beggar woman with a liking for port, suddenly disappeared. Other old ladies vanished, and Burke and Hare began to lure in unknown travellers, making them drunk and then suffocating them.

Then the two men, aided by their wives, became greedier and careless: they picked on eighteen-year-old Mary Petersen and, after smothering her, delivered her body to the medical school. How were they to know that Mary was intimately acquainted with some of the students, who recognized her corpse?

But other murders followed. Burke and Hare were finally apprehended with the corpse of Margery Docherty and thrown into jail. Hare, who was the brains behind the scheme, turned king's evidence and he and his wife were eventually set free. Burke was found guilty and sentenced to death. The number of murders the pair committed was never known exactly, estimates range from sixteen to thirty. On Burke's way to the gallows the people watching shouted out, 'Burke him, Burke him,' and the phrase stuck. It is ironic that by some accounts Burke's own body was later dissected at a public lecture – but not, however, by Dr Knox!

Busby

A tall bearskin hat worn by certain regiments of the British Army. This piece of headwear is generally believed to have been named after the strict disciplinarian headmaster of Westminster School, Richard Busby (1606–95). Amongst his pupils were Dryden, Locke and Christopher Wren.

A *busby* was also a particularly large and bushy wig of this period and the resemblance may have caused the hat to be so described.

Caesarean
Caius Julius assumed his dynastic name of Caesar as part of his birthright. He was delivered into the world via a section cut (Latin *caedere*) through his mother's abdomen, and today all such births are called *caesareans*.

Camellia
A broad-leaved flowering evergreen shrub of the tea family native to Asia and noted for its waxy, rose-like blooms.

Georg Josef Kamel, also know as Camellus (1661–1706), was a Moravian Jesuit who went to the Philippines as a missionary. In the grounds of the Jesuit college of Manila he planted a herb garden and used its crop to augment the little pharmacy that he opened for poor Filipinos. Kamel kept careful records of his plants' growth and development, which he regularly sent to London to be published in the *Philosophical Transactions* of the Royal Society. Linnaeus, who classified nearly every plant we known today, named the camellia after him.

Cant
Hypocritically pious language, jargon.

Andrew Cant (1590–1663) was a Presbyterian minister in Aberdeen who is reputed to have had such a strange way of delivering sermons that only his local congregation had any idea of what he was talking about, let alone if he was sincere. The name has stuck for all ravings of this kind in the name of religion.

Beggars were known as *the canting crew* in earlier times, but this probably derived from the whining noise they made (from the Latin *cantus*, a song).

Cardigan
The knitted woollen waistcoat, with or without sleeves, was named after the Seventh Earl of Cardigan, James Thomas Brudenell (1797–1868). Originally known as the Cardigan

jacket, the garment was first worn by British soldiers against the bitter cold of the Crimean winter. Lord Cardigan was the leader of the Light Brigade in the famous and disastrous charge on Balaclava in 1854. That battle was the source of the name for the knitted woollen hat which the soldiers favoured, the *balaclava*. Cardigan survived the battle and was lionized on his return to England, dying later in a riding accident at his home in Northamptonshire.

Casanova

A *casanova* is a man with a reputation for lust and amorous escapades. The word derives from Giovanni Jacopo (or Giacono) Casanova de Siengalt (1725–98), who secured his reputation as an amorist by writing lengthy memoirs. Born in Venice, the son of an actor, Casanova went to a seminary, but his immoral behaviour soon caused the monks to expel him. After that he spent a short spell in the service of Cardinal Acquaviva in Rome, became a soldier and a professional violinist, and then wandered round the capitals of Europe, mixing with the wealthy aristocracy. Blessed with good looks and more than his fair share of charm, Casanova was accepted wherever he went; he would pretend to be a diplomat, a preacher, a professional gambler, even at times an alchemist. Hostesses and fathers soon discovered the other side of his personality and Casanova was condemned, through his insatiable lust, to spend his life on the move. He eventually settled down as secretary and librarian to Count von Waldstein of Bohemia and it was at this time that he wrote his memoirs (in twelve volumes), first published in 1822.

Catherine wheel

The brightly coloured, spinning fireworks were named after Saint Catherine of Alexandria. The firework's movement evokes the reputed martyrdom of this young virgin of noble descent, whose memory is celebrated on 25 November. The story goes that having protested against Christian persecutions during the reign of Emperor Maximinus (early fourth century AD), she was sentenced to be broken on a spiked wheel. However, miraculously, it was the wheel that broke. Catherine was eventually beheaded, the angels carrying her body to Mount Sinai where it was found 400 years later and a monastery built in her memory. She ceased to be officially recognized by the Church in 1969 due to doubts concerning her existence.

St Catherine also gave her name to a circular window with radiating spokes.

Celsius

Anders Celsius (1701–44) was a Swedish astronomer and the inventor of the centigrade, or *Celsius*, temperature scale. He was born in Uppsala, where he was later to become professor of astronomy. In 1742 he devised the scale which simplified the earlier Fahrenheit scale by dividing the temperature between boiling point and freezing point into a hundred equal parts. Initially, Celsius set the boiling point of water at 0 degrees and the freezing point at 100 degrees. After his death, the scale was reversed to give what we know today as centigrade measurements.

Chauvinism

Exaggerated patriotism. In the last decade the usage of the word has been vastly increased by the women's liberation movement and the term *male chauvinist* – to describe one who advocates male supremacy – has crept into the language. The word *chauvinism* – which in its original sense means an extreme sense of patriotism – dates from the days of the first French Republic.

Nicolas Chauvin (*fl.* 1815) of Rochefort was a soldier in Napoleon's army. Many times wounded, he became the laughing stock of his peers because of his fanatical devotion to Napoleon, which verged on idolatry. In compensation for his injuries, Napoleon awarded him a ceremonial sabre, a red ribbon and a pension of 200 francs (about £20) a year. Despite such meagre recognition Chauvin continued to be Napoleon's slave, considering the reward to be generous.

The Cogniard brothers in their famous vaudeville, *La Cocarde Tricolore*, produced in Paris in 1831, alluded to the characteristics of Chauvin when they included the line, '*Je suis français, je suis Chauvin*'. The character subsequently appeared in a number of works, including Charet's *Conscript Chauvin* and *The Scarlet Pimpernel* by Baroness Orczy. The word was soon used on both sides of the English Channel for any kind of ultra-nationalism.

Chesterfield

The term *chesterfield*, to describe a type of sofa, usually leather and with a buttoned, cushioned back and sides, derives from the Fourth Earl of Chesterfield, Philip Dormer Stanhope (1694–1773), who first devised that style of seat.

Chesterfield was an ambassador and statesman, who served at The Hague and in Ireland as Viceroy. However, it is for his *Letters*, which he wrote to his son Philip, that he is chiefly remembered. They were not written for publication but were rather the letters of a caring father. They were intended to tell the boy about worldliness, power, ambition . . . and women. There were some 400 in all and he wrote a further 300 to his godson when Philip died in 1768.

Johnson was later to describe Chesterfield's *Letters* as teaching the 'morals of a whore and the manners of a dancing master', but Johnson was not entirely unbiased. Several years earlier, while he was in the process of compiling his dictionary, he had sought patronage and financial help from the earl. Chesterfield gave him £10 and then failed in his patronage for seven years. On the appearance of the dictionary, Chesterfield commended it highly, thus incurring Johnson's wrath in this hypocrisy.

Clerihew

A humorous four-lined rhyming poem which does not scan. Clerihews are usually biographical and often make some satirical statement about the person whose name appears in the first line.

When Edmund Clerihew Bentley (1875–1956) was a sixteen-year-old schoolboy at St Paul's, in London, he jotted down these lines in a science class:

> *Sir Humphrey Davy*
> *Abominated gravy,*
> *He lived in the odium*
> *Of having discovered sodium.*

The first example of this type of verse was thus committed to paper.

Bentley began professional life as a journalist on the *Daily News* and later joined the *Daily Telegraph*. He made a name for himself with his fictitious detective Trent, modelled on Sherlock Holmes, but far more fallible. The type of verse to which he has left his name was first introduced in his book *Biography for Beginners* (1905).

Another notable clerihew is:

> *Sir Christopher Wren*
> *Said, 'I am going to dine with some men.*
> *If anyone calls,*
> *Say I am designing St Paul's.'*

Cocktail

The origins of this word describing a mixed, alcoholic aperitif have been lengthily disputed. One fanciful and charming theory justifies its inclusion here. In legend, the Aztec princess Xochitl is said to have given such a drink – concocted from fruit juices and spirits – to a king she loved. Other derivations give its origin in the name of a mixed drink from the wine-growing district of the Gironde known as *coquetel*, or base it loosely on the fact that a horse with its tail docked or not a pure breed is called a *cocktail*.

Codswallop

Codswallop is nowadays a term used to describe any remark or theory that is thought to be nonsense. However, the expression originates from Hiram Codd, who in *c*. 1870 designed a bottle which was closed by means of a glass marble stuck in the neck. The marble was held in place by the pressure from a fizzy drink inside the bottle. *Wallop* in those days was the slang name for beer, so *codswallop* was used to refer to a beer bottle that was closed in this fashion.

Colt

A repeating pistol. Colt revolvers pop up in the hands of many heroes and villains of twentieth-century crime literature as well as Wild West personalities such as Jesse James and Wild Bill Hickock. The inventor of the gun – Colonel Samuel Colt (1814–62) – became a legend in the West on the strength of his celebrated six-shooter.

Born in Connecticut, at the age of sixteen Colt ran away to sea; while aboard ship, he carved a wooden model of the revolver. In 1835 he patented his gun, which soon went into mass production, making him one of the wealthiest men in America. Colt's revolver was a single-barrel pistol with a rotating breech containing six bullets; it came into its own in the Mexican War of 1846–48.

Colt, who made money marketing weapons of death, was himself addicted to nitrous oxide, laughing gas.

Comstockery

The suppression of potentially corrupting literature. In England there was Bowdler; in America it was Anthony Comstock. Comstock (1844–1915) devoted most of his life to the vigorous suppression of all plays and books that he thought to be corrupting, driving a number of publishers out of business. He also led the New York Society for the Suppression of Vice. George Bernard Shaw coined the word *comstockery* in 1905 to describe such practices and gave Mr Comstock his dubious immortality.

Couéism

A school of psychotherapy, founded by Emile Coué (1857–1926). Couéism gave us one phrase that has recently enjoyed something of a revival amongst the 'me' generation. 'Every day, in every way, I am becoming better and better' was the key phrase of Coué's teaching. Using the power of autosuggestion, he would encourage his patients to repeat this phrase over and over again – in the hope that thinking is believing and believing can make a reality.

Crap

To *crap* is to defecate and derives from Crapper's Valveless Water Waste Preventor which was the name under which the first flush lavatory was sold in England. The inventor, the sanitary engineer Thomas Crapper, who was born in Thorne, near Doncaster, in 1837, delivered England from the miserable inconvenience of the chamber pot and garderobe and, in the process, gave the English language a series of spin-off words and expressions. For example, *it's a load of crap* describes anything considered rubbish. To be *crapped on from a great height* signifies a spectacular and somewhat contemptuous punishment, and one which is often publicly embarrassing. *Crappy* describes that which is substandard.

Crapps

The name of a popular American gambling game, played with dice, originates from the nickname of a a Frenchman, Bernard Marigny, who introduced dice-playing to New Orleans at the beginning of the nineteenth century. His nickname was Johnny Crapaud, which means 'Johnny Toad' – a name applied to all Frenchmen in the USA in the early 1800s.

Croesus

As rich as Croesus denotes enormous wealth.

Croesus was the last king of Lydia (*c*. 560–546BC). His fortune was so huge and became so legendary that his name has become associated with vast riches. He considered himself a very happy man, so much so that when Solon, the Athenian law-giver, visited him, Croesus asked him if he knew of anyone happier. Solon replied, 'Call no man happy until he is dead,' by which he did not mean that earthly happiness is impossible, rather that catastrophe can befall even the most secure and cheerful of men. When Cyrus defeated Lydia and Croesus was condemned to die by burning at the stake, he had good cause to remember Solon's words. As he approached the pyre, Croesus called upon Solon, and his captor then charitably pardoned him.

Curry favour, to

To curry favour is to seek advancement by ingratiating oneself with the powerful and influential. Nothing to do with Indian cooking, its origin can actually be traced to a French satirical poem of the Middle Ages, the *Roman de Favel*. Favel (or Fauvel) is the name of a horse (the word in French means chestnut-coloured) owned by the king and is groomed by everyone to get into the king's good books. To brush a horse is to *curry* it. The phrase was originally *to curry Favel*.

Daguerreotype

Louis Jacques Mandé Daguerre (1789–1851) was a French painter and physicist who pioneered the first practical photographic process which now bears his name.

Before he began his scientific and artistic work, Daguerre was a government revenue official and a landscape and theatrical scenery painter. He made friends with the physicist J. N. Niepce (1765–1833), who had long been investigating the possibilities of photography and together they developed a process which produced an image with the help of the action of sunlight. It involved the use of a metal plate treated with iodine of silver; the plate was developed in mercury vapour. After Niepce's death in 1833 Daguerre perfected the process, producing his first results in 1839 for which he was awarded the Légion d'Honneur.

Dahlia

One of the eighteen species of tuberous rooted plants of the thistle family. The dahlia, for a long time a favourite flower of the Aztecs, was unknown in Europe until the eighteenth century. It was discovered by Humboldt in Mexico in 1789 and sent to Professor Cavanilles of the botanic garden in Madrid and named after the celebrated Swedish botanist Anders Dahl following his death in that year. The dahlia was first introduced into the UK in 1798 by the Marchioness of Bute. Some say the plant was named after Dahl because of the absurd resemblance between the shaggy bloom of the plant and the unkempt hair which the doctor had sported.

Dandie Dinmont

The small grey or brown, curly-haired, working terrier with long body and short strong legs known as a *Dandie Dinmont* was named after a character in Walter Scott's *Guy Mannering* (1815). In the novel Dandie Dinmont was a friendly and sturdy old farmer who lived in Liddesdale in the Scottish Lowlands. Scott is presumed to have based his character on James Davidson of Hindlee, who was just such a farmer. In the book Dinmont is portrayed as being the proud owner of a breed of terriers. So, in reality, was Davidson, who named his dogs Mustard or Pepper according to their colour.

Darby and Joan

This affectionate term for a long- and happily married couple first appeared in a ballad by Henry Woodfall published in the *Gentleman's Magazine* in 1735. As a boy, Woodfall was apprentice to a London printer called John Darby (d. 1730). Woodfall obviously was deeply fond of the old man and his wife – Joan – and gave them unlooked-for immortality when he wrote about them.

Davenport

Davenports are narrow, vertically folding writing desks, with side drawers and pigeonholes under the table flap. The hinged writing surface can be lifted upwards to lie flat when not in use. The first davenport was made to the specifications of a Captain Davenport, who commissioned the Lancashire firm Gillow to execute his design *c*. 1820–40.

A *davenport* is also a large kind of sofa, often convertible into a bed, designed a little later.

Derby

A general term for any kind of flat race with an open field of contestants.

The most famous derby, of course, is that held every year on the first Wednesday in June at Epsom Downs in Surrey. Open only to three-year-old colts and fillies (unusual at its first introduction, as most races were for older horses), no horse can ever win the 1½-mile race twice – by definition. The race was named after Edward Stanley, Twelfth Earl of Derby (1752–1834), who first proposed it in 1780. The story goes that but for the toss of a coin the competition could have been called the Hawkewood Stakes, as Sir John Hawkewood was also instrumental in introducing it. However, though Sir John lost the toss, his horse beat Derby's in the first race.

Another major derby run annually is that run at Churchill Downs in Louisville, Kentucky, in the USA, but the name has now been applied to all kinds of open events from donkey derbies to the so-called 'demolition derbies' involving stock cars.

Earl Derby also gave his name to a type of bowler hat.

Derrick

The word *derrick* describing a form of crane in which the
distance from the end of the jib to the pillar can be changed
derives from the name of a seventeenth-century Tyburn
hangman. Derrick, who served under the Provost Marshal
in the Earl of Essex's expedition to Cadiz, is said to have
performed over 3000 executions. He was also responsible
for modifications and 'improvements' to the basic gallows
structure.

While he was in Cadiz, Derrick was charged with rape
and found guilty. He was sentenced to death – by hanging –
but at the last minute he was pardoned and returned to
England to become chief hangman.

Ironically, it was Derrick who pulled the rope on Essex
himself. In a contemporary ballad, 'Essex's Good Night',
twenty-three executions by the notorious Derrick are
mentioned and the ballad concludes with the lines:

> *By now thou seest myself is come,*
> *By chance into thy hands I light.*
> *Strike out thy blow, that I may know*
> *Thou Essex loved at his good-night.*

Derringer

This short-barrelled, large-bore pocket pistol immortalizes
Henry Deringer (1786–1869). He was a Philadelphia
gunsmith who began making pistols in 1825, but eventually
specialized in one he had invented. Its immediate
popularity made copying inevitable and one successful
manufacturer began to market a *derringer*, having inserted
an extra *r* in its name to avoid patent and copyright laws. In
the end, it was the spelling of the wildcat version that stuck.

Abraham Lincoln was assassinated by a bullet from a
derringer fired by John Wilkes Booth in 1865.

Diddle

The word *diddle* – the slang description of a petty swindle –
stems from a character in James Kenney's first play, *Raising
the Wind* (1803). Jeremy Diddler, the hero of the farce, was
an imaginative petty crook who 'raised the wind' by
continually borrowing small amounts of money which he

never paid back. The success of the play, which opened in London in 1803, soon led to the adoption of *diddle* to describe such practice. Kenny, who was born in Ireland in 1780, wrote a number of successful plays and farces, which enjoyed popularity long after his death in 1849.

The verb *to diddle* was given a firm position in the English language when Edgar Allan Poe wrote an essay entitled 'Diddling Considered as One of the Exact Sciences'.

Diesel
A type of internal combustion engine.

Rudolf Diesel (1858–1913) was the son of a German couple who lived in Paris until the Franco-Prussian War of 1870 forced them to flee to England. They had scarcely arrived when a message came from the young boy's uncle, offering to look after him until the war was over. Rudolf was hastily dispatched back to the Continent – a lonely, uncomfortable journey that took eight days.

In later life he was to remember this slow trip. He determined to do something to improve transport. He thought that the inefficient steam engine could be replaced by something better. After studying engineering at Augsburg and Munich Diesel applied for a patent for an improvement of the internal combustion engine. Diesel's design was based on the idea, proposed by the French scientist Carnot in 1824, that instead of electrically igniting the mixture in the cylinder head, the heat generated by the compression itself could do the trick. Thus, the principle was that the piston would compress air in the cylinder at many times the pressure in a standard combustion engine, and then fuel would be injected, leading to a spontaneous explosion. Diesel constructed his new version, but nearly died when the machine blew up in his face due to the tremendous pressure inside. In his diary he had noted, 'The birth of an idea is the happy moment in which everything appears possible and reality has not yet entered into the problem.'

However, his experiment had proved that a compression-ignition engine would work; the problem was to perfect it and to determine the most suitable type of fuel. For years Diesel tried everything, from alcohol to peanut oil

. . . until he finally hit on a semi-refined crude oil, which was also cheap. His patent was granted in 1892 and the first commerically successful engine was completed in 1897. As it can run on much lower grade fuel than the petrol engine and uses only 66 per cent as much, the diesel became very popular and the inventor rich and famous. He even discussed the possibilities of powering Count Zeppelin's dirigibles with diesel – a project which eventually came to fruition but not till both men were dead. Today diesel engines are a major source of industrial power.

Diesel died a curious death: on a voyage to London he disappeared overboard, on a September evening in 1913. His corpse was fished from the water ten days later.

Dinnyhayser

An Australian term to describe a knockout blow in boxing. The word originated from an Australian prizefighter Dinny Hayes, who had an awesome reputation for delivering mighty punches.

Doily

These small ornamental napkins used on cake dishes, etc., usually made out of paper and resembling lace, were invented by a Mr Doily (whose name may also have been spelled Doiley, Doyly or Doyley), a linen draper during the reign of Queen Anne. His shop in the Strand sold fabrics which were trimmed with lace embroidery or crochet work. In the 24 January 1712 issue of the *Spectator*, Dryden refers to 'Doyley's petticoats' in a wry essay entitled 'The Ways to Raise a Man's Fortune, or the Art of Growing Rich'. He continues, 'The famous Doily is still fresh in everyone's memory, who raised a fortune by finding out materials for such stuffs as might at once be cheap and genteel. I have heard it affirmed, that had he not discovered this frugal method of gratifying our pride, we should hardly have been so well able to carry on the last war.'

Don Juan

The archetype of all rakes, libertines and heartless seducers, Don Juan was the legendary son of a noble Seville family of the Middle Ages. He first appeared in a Spanish tragedy, *The Rake of Seville*, by Tirso de Molina (1630), but

the stories about him are legion and he has been the subject
for many operas and plays, including Mozart's *Don
Giovanni*, in which we hear the valet, Leporello, telling of his
master's '700 mistresses in Italy, in Germany 800, in
Turkey and France 91, in Spain 1003'. Other writers have
used Don Juan as a character in their works – Byron,
Molière, Dumas (père) and Shaw in *Man and Superman*.

Doubting Thomas

This expression signifying one who will not believe until he
sees for himself is an allusion to St Thomas, the apostle, who
lost his faith in Christ. He expressed his doubts by saying,
'How know we the way?' (John 14:5). After the
Resurrection, when the other disciples were convinced that
they had seen Christ risen from the dead, Thomas said,
'Except that I shall see in his hands the print of the nails,
and put my finger into the print of the nails, and thrust my
hand into his side. I will not believe' (John 20:25).

Draconian

Draco was significant in that in 621 BC he codified and wrote
down for the first time the laws of Athens – formerly
interpreted arbitrarily by the elders. However, his new
penal code was so harsh in its punishments that his name,
and the adjective *draconian*, are now associated with any
laws of unreasonable severity. His list made punishable by
death almost every offence known to Athenians of his day
– even laziness, petty theft and urinating in public. The
orator, Demades, said that Draco's code was 'written in
blood'. However, one benefit of the laws was to make
redress for homicide the responsibility of the state, thus
avoiding blood feuds between families, and when Solon
repealed most of the Draconian code early in the following
century this was one of the few laws to be kept.

Dunce

The word *dunce* – used to describe anyone who is extremely
stupid – derives from the great medieval Scottish
philosopher and theologian John Duns Scotus
(1256–1308), who was given his curious Christian name
because of his birthplace in Scotland.

The young Duns Scotus entered a Scottish Franciscan friary at the age of fifteen and proved himself an apt pupil and became a priest in 1291. He later went to Oxford, and then lectured abroad, settling in Paris.

During his years at Oxford and Paris, Scotus took issue with the doctrines of Thomas Aquinas. His philosophy included an incorporation of the teaching of Aristotle into Christian theology – but with numerous additions of his own. He was nicknamed 'the Subtle Doctor' (as opposed to Aquinas, known as 'the Angelic Doctor').

Scotus had many followers, who called themselves Dunsmen, Dunses or Scotists. Like him, they involved themselves in hairsplitting over the finer points of divinity, and they were reluctant to accept change. According to Tyndal, 'The old barking curs raged in every pulpit' when new thoughts were introduced. Thus any opponent to progress or learning was called a *dunce* and eventually by implication stupid.

Duns Scotus was buried in Cologne. His epitaph read:

> *Scotia me genuit,*
> *Anglia me suscepit,*
> *Gallia me docuit,*
> *Colonia me tenet.*

Epicure

A person whose happiness derives from refined sensual pleasures.

Epicurus, from whom we derive the common words *epicure* and *epicurean*, was a Greek philosopher born in Samos *c*. 340 BC. He founded a school of philosophy in Athens, where he taught ethics, logic and physics, his pupils living together on his property and including, unusually for that period, slaves and women. His teachings have been distorted by his detractors, who claim that his basic principle was that satisfaction and gratification from high living were the aim of life.

In fact, Epicurus was a man of high moral standing; he set great store by happiness and even regarded virtue as worthless if it did not also produce an agreeable life. 'When we maintain that pleasure is an end, we do not mean the pleasures of profligates and those that consist in sensuality . . . but freedom from pain in the body and from trouble in the mind. For it is not continuous drinkings, nor the satisfaction of lusts . . . but sober reasoning, searching out the motives for all choice and avoidance' (Letter to Menoecus).

Epicurus died *c*. 270 BC.

Everest

This word, meaning the highest point, derives from Sir George Everest (1790–1866), Surveyor General of India, who was responsible for the first comprehensive and detailed maps of the subcontinent, including the Himalayas. The world's highest mountain (29,028 feet) was named after him. The first successful ascent of Everest was achieved on 29 May 1953, by Colonel John Hunt's party, with the New Zealander Edmund Hillary and Sherpa Tensing Norkay reaching the summit. By an amazing coincidence news of the event reached the outside world on the same day as the coronation of Queen Elizabeth II.

Fahrenheit

The thermometric scale giving the freezing point of water as 32 degrees and boiling point as 212 degrees.

At the beginning of the eighteenth century there were almost as many systems of measuring temperatures in Europe as there were men measuring them. But by the end of the century there were, for all useful purposes, only three, one of them being the Fahrenheit scale.

Gabriel Daniel Fahrenheit (1686–1736) was born in Danzig but he moved to Amsterdam when he was orphaned at the age of fifteen. He studied meteorology, and by the age of twenty he had made his first thermometer. In his earliest thermometers he used alcohol, but he soon switched to mercury, fixing the freezing point at 32 degrees in order to avoid minus readings. The division of his scale depended on three fixed points: 0, the point at which the liquid stood

when the tube was placed in ice, water and sea salt; 32
degrees, the level when the tube stood in ice and water
alone, deemed freezing point; and 96 degrees, this third
point being arrived at by placing the tube in the mouth of a
healthy man (this is nowadays judged to be 98·4° F). Thus
the entire scale was divided into 96 equal parts; boiling
point at 212 degrees was fixed only after Fahrenheit's death.
Fahrenheit noted a few difficulties with the system, the
main one being 'the temperature will reach 128 or 132
degrees. Whether these degrees are high enough for the
hottest fevers I have not examined; I do not think, however,
that the degrees named will ever be exceeded in any fever.'
He was, of course, right.

Fahrenheit was elected a Fellow of the Royal Society in
1724.

Fallopian tube

The *fallopian tubes* connect the ovaries of the female
mammals to the womb and were named after the Italian
Gabriel Fallopius (1523–62), also known as Gabriello
Fallopio. Born in Modena, Fallopius was originally
destined for an ecclesiastical career but turned to medicine,
becoming professor of anatomy at Pisa 1548 to 1551, after
which he went to teach at Padua University. He remained
head of the anatomy department there until his early death.

Fanny Adams

Fanny Adams was the nickname given by the Royal Navy in
the nineteenth century to rations of tinned mutton. The
name derived from a gruesome source. In 1812, young
Fanny Adams was murdered; her body was dismembered
and the pieces thrown into the river at Alton, in Hampshire.
The sailors drew a morbidly fanciful comparison. *Sweet
Fanny Adams*, meaning nothing at all, also derives from this
source.

Ferris wheel

Ferris wheels are the enormous power-driven revolving
wheels with carriages that are a prime attraction at summer
fairgrounds. The first ferris wheel was built for the World's
Columbian Exposition in Chicago in 1893 as a rival to the

Eiffel Tower, by G. W. Gale Ferris (1859–96), an engineer
from Galesburg, Illinois. As the wheel revolved on its
stationary axle, the carriages remained parallel to the
ground, affording its passengers a marvellous view of the
fairground. The first wheel stood 250 feet high and carried
thirty-six individual cars, each one of which could seat
up to forty people. The largest ever ferris wheel was built
in London in 1894 and was 328 feet high and could
carry 1200 passengers in forty cars. The ferris wheels
today are not so grand; modern cars seat six to eight
people only.

Forrest fir

The name *forrest fir*, used to designate a particular type of fir
tree now common in the British Isles, does not in fact derive
from *forest*, but from George Forrest of Falkirk, who was
born in 1873 and introduced the species to Britain. He was a
botanist who spent twenty-eight years in China collecting
and cataloguing plants and seeds, and shipping those he
thought of special interest home. He died in Yunan
Province while shooting snipe, but before his death he had
shipped home two mule-loads of seeds – including some of
the forrest fir. Other plants which owe their British
existence to his diligence are the rhododendron, tea plant,
aster and primula.

Freudian slip

To make a *Freudian slip* is to reveal something of one's
unconscious feelings by mistake. The expression is often
used to describe an accidental remark which may be taken
to be more truthful than the word or phrase which the
speaker had intended. Thus, for a husband to call his wife
'mother', or for someone to murmur the name of an old
flame while embracing a new one, could be called a
Freudian slip. To give an out-of-date telephone number
when being asked to supply one's current number could be
said to reveal a desire to return to the place and time when
the old digits were correct. The expression derives from the
teachings of Sigmund Freud (1856–1939), the father of
modern psychoanalysis, whose ideas, much plundered and
distorted, have become widely discussed by those both

inside and outside his profession. The Freudian slip, also known by its technical name of 'partapraxis', includes not only *lapsus linguae* but slips of the pen, misreading, etc. The topic is discussed in Freud's book *The Psychopathology of Everyday Life* (1914).

Fuchsia

These ornamental shrubs with drooping flowers, often a characteristic splendid pink, are found principally in Mexico and the Andes region of South America, although two species are known to be indigenous to New Zealand. A member of the evening primrose family, altogether over fifty varieties are known. They were first introduced into Europe by the German writer and botanist, Leonhard Fuchs (1501–66), formerly professor of medicine specializing in medical plants at Tubingen University. The fuchsia was named in his honour in 1703 by its discoverer Charles Plumier.

Fudge

To fudge an issue means to make light of it, or in some manner to obscure the truth. Benjamin Disraeli's father, Isaac D'Israeli, is reported to have unearthed a seventeenth-century pamphlet which explains the origins of the word thus: 'There was in our time one Captain Fudge, commander of a merchantman (the *Black Eagle*), who upon his return from a voyage, how ill fraught soever his ship was, always brought home to his owners a good crop of lies; so much that now, aboard ship, the sailors when they hear a great lie told, cry out, "You fudge it." ' The captain himself even earned the nickname 'Lying Fudge'.

Furphy

A *furphy* is an unreliable report. The expression, which is Australian slang, stems from the First World War, when containers for sanitary purposes were supplied to Australian military camps by the company Furphy and Co. of Shepparton, Victoria. The name appeared on the side of all the portable lavatories and buckets manufactured by the company, and this led to the troops adopting the word to describe war news derived from latrine rumour, and hence especially dubious.

Another possible derivation is from Joseph Furphy (1843–1912), an Australian author who wrote tall stories under the pseudonym 'Tom Collins'.

Gaga

To describe someone as *gaga* is to imply that he is mentally unbalanced. Possibly the word derives from the French word *gaga*, meaning a foolish old man, though there could be a connection with the Impressionist painter Paul Gauguin (1848–1903). Signs of mental disturbance were present in Gauguin's work and life, and there is a theory that *gaga* is eponymously derived from him.

Galvanize

To stimulate into action by shock, electric or otherwise. Luigi Galvani, the Italian physiologist, was born at Bologna in 1737 and became professor of anatomy at the university there in 1762. There are many versions of the story of how he first came to experiment with animal tissue and electricity, thereby initiating the study of electrophysiology and leaving his mark on the English language with the verb *to galvanize*.

Possibly the most charming of these has the professor lovingly preparing frogs' legs for his sick wife's dinner. While he was dismembering the frogs in the kitchen, he noticed that when he touched the animal tissue with cutlery made from two different metals (e.g. iron and copper), the muscles twitched and the frogs' legs kicked. The professor was amazed. After further experiment he concluded that animal tissue, alive or dead, must generate electricity and that it only needed earthing through the metal conductors to make this apparent. He thus postulated a theory of 'animal electricity'. However, it was not until some years later that the true explanation for the twitching phenomenon was found. It was caused, so Volta discovered, by the fact that electric currents are produced by chemical actions on certain metals. Galvani was not

earthing the frog's own charge – he was turning it into a
battery!

Galvani died in 1798.

Gardenia

An evergreen shrub native to Asia and Tropical Africa,
with beautiful fragrant white flowers. Alexander Garden
(1730–91) discovered a number of species of both flora and
fauna, including the conger eel, named *Amphiuma* by
Linnaeus. His own name has lived on in the flowering
shrub, *gardenia*.

Garden was an American physician of Scottish
extraction who lived in Clarkston, South Carolina, and
made a good living tending to the whims and fancies of
well-to-do ladies. His great interest was botany and he
deplored living so far from the other eminent
eighteenth-century botanists, who were mainly in Europe.
The gardenia was introduced into Europe from the Cape of
Good Hope by the botanist and scholar Richard Warner,
and named for Garden by Linnaeus in 1760.

Gargantuan

Anything, especially an appetite, of huge proportions.
Gargantua was a good giant of medieval or possibly Celtic
legend connected with the Arthurian stories and used by
Rabelais in his famous satire *Gargantua and Pantagruel*,
written in 1534. In this book Gargantua, as a child, needed
the milk of 17,913 cows to satisfy him, and on one occasion
he ate six pilgrims in a salad – staves and all. Gargantua's
own name derives from the word for gullet.

Garibaldi

Garibaldis are red shirts, as sported by Guiseppe Garibaldi
and his followers.

The great Italian patriot (1807–82) was first a sailor but
soon allied himself with the Young Italy movement. Several
times he fled the country or was exiled. He fought for
Sardinia against Austria (1859) and later led an expedition
against the Sicilies, becoming briefly dictator of Sicily.
When Francis II invaded Naples in 1860, Garibaldi
returned to Italy and routed the interloper.

During a brief period of exile from Italy, Garibaldi lived in South America. It was there that the famous 'redshirts' came into existence. While Garibaldi was raising an Italian force in Montevideo, to aid the Montevideans in their war with Buenos Aires, an enormous number of red woollen shirts came onto the market. They were very cheap, and the government of Uruguay bought them up and presented them to Garibaldi and the Italian Legion – 1000 troops – as a gift.

As well as the blouses that perpetuated Garibaldi's name, a currant biscuit, also colourfully known as a 'squashed fly' because of its appearance, was named after him as he had a particular liking for pastries with currants in them.

Gatling gun

The *Gatling gun* was the (originally six-barrelled) crank-operated prototype of the modern machine-gun. Its inventor, Richard Jordan Gatling (1818–1903), of North Carolina, was successful as a designer of agricultural machinery. During the American Civil War, he invented his gun, which he patented in 1862. It was capable of delivering 350 rounds a minute and was both fired and rotated by the crank at the back. However, the gun was initially rejected as being neither efficient nor useful, and the war was practically over the by the time it was officially adopted. It was first used during the siege of St Petersburg (1864–65) and it is said that Custer might have survived Little Big Horn had he not deliberately left his Gatling guns behind.

Also known as a *gat*, the gun was made obsolete by the introduction of the machine-gun, though the principle has been revived in recent years for use on supersonic fighter aircraft.

Geiger counter

An instrument for detecting and measuring radioactivity.

Hans Wilhelm Geiger (1882–1945) was born at Neustadt-an-der-Hardt. He worked under the great scientist Ernest Rutherford at Manchester from 1906 to 1912. While Rutherford made enormous strides towards splitting the atom, Geiger devoted himself to designing an instrument for detecting alpha particles. This, developed originally with Rutherford's help in 1911, became the basis of the modern Geiger counter, a device capable of reading and measuring the rate of radioactive disintegration. Perfected in association with Wilhelm Müller in 1928, it is more properly known as the Geiger–Müller counter.

Georgette

A thin silk crepe fabric, of very fine texture, named after a French dressmaker, Mme Georgette de la Plante. She lived and worked in Paris in the nineteenth century.

Gerrymander

To gerrymander is to divide states or districts into voting areas which will result in unfair advantage being given to one party in an election. The word is also often used to describe mildly manipulative cunning or general fixing.

Elbridge Gerry was born in 1744, the son of a wealthy Massachusetts merchant family. Under the influence of Samuel Adams, he was goaded towards revolutionary ideas at odds with his background and future career. It was a contradiction that he was never to resolve, believing on the one hand in democracy but continuing to lead an aristocratic life himself. The conflict made him touchy, obstinate and difficult.

Gerry was opposing British rule in America long before the Boston Tea Party. He advocated revolution and used his influence to gather supplies for the Continental Army. At the age of thirty-two, he was elected to the Continental Congress and, after several tumultuous years in politics, retired to Massachusetts; but when, two year later, France seized several American ships, John Adams, then President, sent Gerry to Paris to obtain redress.

There were two others on the mission, but Gerry felt that he alone could prevent the impending war. Talleyrand seized on him as the man most likely to negotiate, and attempted to make a secret deal with him. Gerry was recalled to Washington in 1797, charged with conniving with the French. He and his family were ostracized and he was kept under surveillance.

Thirteen years later (1810) he ran for Governor of Massachusetts and won. But his contradictory behaviour continued to cause problems. Gerry soon lost popularity. In his second term of office, in an attempt to keep power, he decided to redraw the voting districts to enable his party (the Republicans) to retain their majority in the imminent election. One day while in the offices of the Boston *Sentinel*, the painter Gilbert Stuart saw a map of the redrawn boundaries on the wall and onto its bizarre shape sketched feet and wings. 'That will do for a salamander,' he declared. 'Better say Gerrymander,' replied the paper's editor, Benjamin Russell. Though this practice was not new, the name stuck.

Gerry eventually became Vice-President of the USA in 1813 but died the following year.

Gibberish

Rapid, inarticulate and foolish talk. According to Dr Johnson this word derives from an alchemist called Geber. Active in the fourteenth century, Geber translated into Latin many of the works of the eighth-century alchemist Jabir ibn Hayyan. In common with the writings of many alchemists, Geber's books tended to be abstruse.

Gimlet

A *gimlet* is a drink created by diluting gin with lime juice. It was believed that neat gin was damaging to the health and organs of naval officers, so in 1890 the British naval surgeon Sir T. O. Gimlette devised the now famous 'healthy' cocktail.

Gladstone bag

The light portmanteau or travelling bag, with a wide mouth folding neatly at the top to close with a central clip, was named after the great statesman and Prime Minister of England, William Ewart Gladstone (1809–98), who frequently carried one.

The bag was not the only thing to which Gladstone lent his name. While Chancellor of the Exchequer in 1860, he cut the import duty payable on cheap French wines. The sudden increase in the amount of wine available caused the name *Gladstone* to be applied for a time to cheap French claret.

A *gladstone* is also a kind of four-wheeled carriage.

Grand Marnier

A liqueur. César Ritz, the hotelier, was approached by a wealthy industrialist, Marnier Lapostolle, a man small in stature, who asked him to name a liqueur of the industrialist's own invention. Ritz tried the drink and found it excellent. Half in irony, perhaps, and half in genuine desire to please a good client, Ritz called the drink *Grand Marnier*.

Grangerize

To illustrate a book by adding prints, etc., cut from other books.

In 1769 a parson of the village of Shiplake in Oxfordshire published a book in six volumes entitled *Biographical History of England from Egbert the Great to the Revolution, Consisting of Characters Dispersed in Different Classes, and Adapted to a Methodical Catalogue of Engraved British Heads*. The author was James Granger, born in 1723, and his book introduced a new concept in the presentation of literary biographies – known today as *grangerizing*.

His idea was that the reader should illustrate the volumes by collecting engraved portraits and pasting them in at appropriate places, blank pages being left for this purpose. The idea caught on, especially among wealthy women with time on their hands and a little artistic flair. Some of the efforts were splendid and the prices of grangerized books more than quadrupled. Many copies of the *Biographical History* are still in existence today, some of which contain thousands of illustrations culled from other sources. Unfortunately, the craze led to the destruction of many valuable books and ephemeral material in the search for engraved portraits. Granger himself was said to have ripped out 14,000 illustrations in this manner.

Granger was well liked in his parish, although his liberal views caused Dr Johnson to say of him, 'The dog is a Whig. I do not much like to see a Whig in any dress, but I hate to see a Whig in a parson's gown.' He was also an outspoken preacher, his most famous sermon being the 'Nature and Extent of Industry', which he later published in book form with the wry dedication 'To the inhabitants of the parish of Shiplake who neglect the service of the church, and spend the Sabbath in the worst kind of idleness, this plain sermon, which they never heard, and probably will never read, is inscribed by their sincere well wisher and faithful minister, J.G.'

Granger died in 1776 of an apoplectic fit while administering the sacrament.

Greengage

This green plum obviously derives part of its name from its hue. *Gage* was added in honour of Sir William Gage, of Hengrave, Suffolk. Introduced into France *c*. 1500, the fruit was originally named *reine-claude* after the wife of Francis I and was renamed in 1725 on its introduction to the UK by Gage.

Grog

Rough liquor. Grogram is a coarse fabric of silk, mohair and wool (from the French *gros grain*, coarse material) and Admiral Sir Edward Vernon (1684–1757) was nicknamed Old Grog because he habitually wore a cloak made from it. In 1740, in an attempt to limit the number of brawls that took place aboard his ships, Vernon issued an order stating that all rations of rum were to be watered down. The sailors dubbed the resulting drink *grog*, a word which later became associated with any cheap liquor.

The term *grog* also gave rise to the adjective *groggy*, probably used first to describe how someone recovering from an excess of alcohol is feeling!

Grog rations were stopped to all ratings on 1 July 1970.

Guillotine

An instrument of execution which consists of a weighted diagonal blade, suspended between two upright posts, that falls from a height and severs the victim's head at the neck.

Instruments similar to the guillotine had been employed for many centuries in Scotland, Germany, Italy and several eastern countries before it was introduced to France – not by Joseph Ignace Guillotin (1738–1814), who, unhappily for him, left his name to the device, but by Dr Antoine Louis (1723–92). In fact, for a time the guillotine was known as the *louisette*.

Guillotin was a French physician and an inventor of medical instruments. He was interested in the louisette because it offered a quick and relatively painless mode of death. When the machine was introduced in France – the first person to be guillotined was a highwayman on 25 April 1792 – it was generally kept for the aristocracy and those who, it was considered, deserved preferential treatment, beheading being reserved only for the upper classes. As a member of the Constituent Assembly, Guillotin proposed that the method should be used for all executions, on humanitarian and egalitarian grounds. At the height of the Reign of Terror, in June and July 1792, when 1376 heads fell, his suggestion was taken up.

Dr Guillotin died quietly in his bed. He had been appalled when the device was named after him and Victor Hugo was later to comment: 'There are unfortunate men; Columbus could not attach his name to discovery, and Guillotin could not detach his from his invention.'

The guillotine is still a legal, though rarely used method of execution in France.

In British parliamentary jargon, *to apply the guillotine* means to curtail a debate by dividing it up and fixing in advance the times at which votes on particular sections must be taken.

In offices and studios a heavy-duty paper cutter with a broad cutting blade is known as a *guillotine*.

Guppy

A species of tiny tropical fish, originally from Venezuela and Trinidad. These popular aquarium fish were named after R. J. Lechmere Guppy, president of the Scientific Association of Trinidad, who discovered them in 1866 and presented specimens to the British Museum in 1868.

Guy

Three words derive from the name *Guy Fawkes*.

Guys, the dummies which can be seen on bonfires every 5 November, are stuffed effigies of one of the men who had the audacity to attempt to blow up the Houses of Parliament on 5 November 1605. Fawkes (1570–1606) was born in York of Protestant parents. From 1593 to 1604 he served as a mercenary in the Spanish army in the Netherlands and then returned to England. He was converted to Catholicism and, incensed by the severity of the penal laws against Catholics imposed by James I, he plotted with several other Catholics to blow up Parliament when the king was there. He was caught redhanded, tortured on the rack, tried and hanged on 31 January 1606.

The second eponym that originated from his name is the verb *to guy*, meaning to mock or make fun of. This sense stems by analogy of the people jeering at Fawkes on his way to the gallows with the crowds that stand round the flaming effigies in the present day.

The origins of the noun *guy*, meaning fellow or chap, have also been traced to Guy Fawkes, although this is disputed.

Ham

The derisory term *ham* is often applied to an inferior actor. The origins of the word are disputed, but the most likely theory seems to be that the word derives from Hamish McCullough (1835–85), who toured with his troupe of actors through Illinois and other Mid-western states of the USA. His company was known as Ham's Actors, after his own nickname, and their performances are reputed to have been dismally bad.

The adjective *hammy* and the phrase *hamming it up* (usually implying deliberate theatrical gesture) derive from the same source.

Another derivation is from the fact that in the nineteenth century ham fat was used to remove theatrical make-up and thus *ham* is an abbreviation of *hamfatter*, meaning an actor. The description was popularized in a Negro minstrel song 'The Ham-fat Man'.

Hansom

The *hansom* cab, predecessor to the black London taxi cab,
was designed and patented by Joseph Hansom. It was said
to make a beautiful woman look like a jewel inside a
velvet-lined casket and Benjamin Disraeli called it the
'gondola of London'.

Hansom (1803–82) was born in York, the son of a joiner.
He was apprenticed in the trade but then studied
architecture. His buildings include Birmingham Town
Hall (1833) and several Catholic churches. A versatile man,
in 1834 he registered a 'Patent Safety Cab'. Hansoms
became immediately popular and though the designs were
modified, they still retained the basic features of Hansom's
original.

Harlot

There is a rather fanciful story that this word, meaning a
prostitute, comes from Arlette, a tanner's daughter from
Falaise, who was surprised naked whilst washing her
clothes by Robert I, Duke of Normandy (d. 1035). The
result was William the Bastard (1027–87), better known as
William the Conqueror. However, a more likely derivation
is from a combination of two Old German words, *Hari*
meaning army and *Lot*, a loiterer. The word *harlot* itself
appears in Middle English as a general word for ruffian or
vagabond of either sex.

Havelock

A *havelock* is a white cloth which hangs down from the back
of a cap and protects the wearer's neck from strong sunlight.
Although nowadays associated with the French Foreign
Legion, the cloth was named after Sir Henry Havelock
(1795–1857), a British soldier who entered the army a
month after Waterloo and arrived in India in 1823. He
married the daughter of a British Baptist missionary and
spent virtually all the rest of his life in India – leaving only
once in thirty-four years to make a brief trip home.

Hobson's choice

Hobson's choice is no choice, 'this or nothing'.

Thomas Hobson (*c.* 1544–1631) was the university

carrier between Cambridge and London. His job was to rent out horses, but he always made one proviso – the customer must take the horse which stood nearest to the stable door. Perhaps the most well-known example of Hobson's choice is Henry Ford's dictum that customers could have cars in any colour they liked so long as it was black.

The *Spectator* of 14 October 1712 explained the expression *Hobson's choice* as follows: 'A vulgar error taken and used, when a man is reduced to an extremity . . . the propriety of the maxim is to use it when you would say there is plenty, but you must make such a choice as to not hurt another who is to come after you.'

Hobson flourished and became a very popular figure in Cambridge, so much so that when he died on 1 January 1631, leaving eight children, Milton wrote two humorous epitaphs and a street was named after him in the town. Harold Brighouse wrote the play *Hobson's Choice*, a comedy of manners and marriage, which has proved enduringly popular.

Hooker

Prostitutes, especially in America, are often called *hookers*, and many stories abound as to how the usage came about. According to one account, they are named after the famous Union general of the American Civil War, Joseph Hooker (1814–79), known as 'Fighting Joe', whose company seemed to attract large numbers of prostitutes. It is also said that Hooker declared the red-light district of Washington DC off-limits to his soldiers, thereby giving his name to the inhabitants of such areas.

Another possible derivation is from the little ships known as *hookers* that traded with the Hook of Holland – a place well-known for its painted ladies.

Hooligan

The origins of the word *hooligan*, used to describe one who indulges in reckless and antisocial behaviour, are not precise. According to the *Oxford English Dictionary*, the term entered the English language in 1898, as a slang word for a street rowdy or ruffian. Partridge in his *Dictionary of Slang* quotes at length from the only reputable source, Clarence Rook, who wrote a book entitled *Hooligan Nights* in 1899.

Rook maintains that there definitely was a man named Patrick Hooligan, who at about this time 'walked to and fro among his fellow men, robbing them and occasionally bashing them'. But, as he says, legend has been at work and it is probable that many of the exploits attributed to Hooligan were in fact products of the imaginations of others.

Patrick Hooligan frequented a pub in Southwark called the Lamb and Flag. He controlled a gang of boys who lived on their wits and were ready for any devilry in return for a reward.

Hoover

The first Hoover vacuum cleaner was produced in 1908 by the Hoover Suction Sweeper Co. Originally the invention of J. Murray Spangler of Ohio, the upright machine's potential was seen by W. H. Hoover who eventually persuaded Spangler to sell him the rights. By 1912 he was exporting his sweepers to the UK where the vacuum cleaner had already been in use for some years.

Hoyle, according to

Until the last century, and occasionally today, the phrase *according to Hoyle* was invoked as a yardstick against which to measure the fairness of any game, or to solve queries arising out of it.

The namesake of the phrase, Edmund Hoyle, was born in 1672. In his book *A Short Treatise on the Game of Whist* (1742), he systematized the rules of whist and set up a standard according to which the game should be played. His authority gradually extended to other card and indoor games (e.g. chess, backgammon, etc.) and, even today, books are published setting out Hoyle's rules. His name has slipped into the English language as a synonym for the correct way of playing a game.

Although little is known of Hoyle's career away from the card table, he is thought to have been a barrister. He died at home in London's Cavendish Square in 1769, aged ninety-seven. Hoyle seems to have been popular in literary

circles and is mentioned in Fielding's *Tom Jones*, Byron's
Don Juan and Alexander Thomson's poem *Whist*.

Jackanapes

A *jackanapes* is a silly, conceited person, a ridiculous upstart.
It was introduced as the nickname of William de la Pole,
Duke of Suffolk (1396–1450). De la Pole served in the
English army and took command when Salisbury died
during the seige of Orleans. However, the success of Jeanne
d'Arc forced him to surrender. On returning to England
and entering a life of politics, de la Pole's machinations soon
made him extremely unpopular and, banished for
conspiring to usurp the throne, he was beheaded in 1450 at
sea whilst going into exile. His armorial badge was an ape
with a ball and chain, and as the slang for a monkey then
was Jack Napes or Jack of Naples, the name came to be
applied to the man himself.

Jack Russell

Jack Russell terriers were originally bred in the West
Country. They were named after the sporting parson, Jack
Russell (1795–1883), who was born in Dartmouth.
Educated at Oxford, he became the curate of Swymbridge,
near Barnstaple. Apart from his clerical duties, Jack Russell
was a keen huntsman, a master of the local foxhounds, and
an all-round sporting country gentleman.

Jacky Howe

These sleeveless shirts worn by sheepshearers in
Queensland, Australia, were named after John Howe
(1855–1922). Howe became a legend in his own lifetime by
creating a record for sheepshearing – 321 merinos in one
working day – in 1892. This record remained until 1950,
when Jacky Howe's ability with his shears was finally
bettered by a machine.

Jekyll and Hyde

To describe someone as a *Jekyll and Hyde* is to suggest that he
is two-faced – someone who can act one way sometimes,
but totally differently at others, the contrast always being

between good and bad behaviour. This two-facedness is not seen as the result of inherent schizophrenia, but rather as a calculated act, usually to cover up dire treacheries.

The Strange Case of Dr Jekyll and Mr Hyde was written by Robert Louis Stevenson in 1886, inspired by the life of William Brodie (1741–88). Brodie was deacon of the Incorporation of Edinburgh Wrights and Masons, a member of the town council and a respected citizen. That was by day. At night, as the leader of a masked gang of robbers, he brought terror and havoc to the very citizens whom by day he championed. He was finally apprehended and sentenced to death by hanging.

Jerry-built

Anything, but particularly a building, which is quickly and shoddily made can be described as *jerry-built*.

The term may be derived from Jericho, the walls of which, according to the Old Testament, fell down at the sound of Joshua's trumpet. An alternative derivation is from the Jerry brothers, who, in the early nineteenth century, ran a Liverpool building firm which used poor materials to put up showy but unsound houses.

Jerrycan

A five-gallon petrol can used in the armed forces. The word may be derived from jeroboam, a large bowl, bottle or goblet. This in turn is derived from Jeroboam I, King of Israel, 931–910 BC. It was he who 'made Israel to sin' (I Kings 14:16). Other sources give the origin of jerrycan from the American slang word *jerry*, meaning a chamber pot.

Joe

Joe is an Australian slang word for policeman, used by the Diggers as an insult to the forces of law and order. The name derives from Charles Joseph La Trobe (1801–75), who was Lieutenant Governor of Victoria in 1851. He was a fanatical lawman, insisting that checks be made on the licences of every digger, or miner, in the state. They resented his interference and nicknamed all police and officials whom they considered petty after him.

John Dory

A spiny-rayed fish found in the Atlantic and growing up to three feet in length. One source cites it as being named after a sixteenth-century privateer called John Dory. It is more likely that the name derives from its colour, which is similar to that of a goldfish (French *doré*, golden); indeed, it used to be known more commonly as the dory. It was from the mouth of this fish that St Peter is supposed to have taken a silver coin to pay the temple tax (Matthew 17:27); on either side of its body there are marks to indicate his thumb- and fingerprints.

Joule

A *joule* is the electrical unit equivalent to the amount of work done or heat generated by a current of 1 ampere acting for 1 second against a resistance of 1 ohm. It is also used to describe units of heat and thus appears instead of calories in some diet sheets.

It was named after James Prescott Joule (1818–89), an English physicist who was born at Salford. He studied chemistry under Dalton and showed experimentally that heat is a form of energy, and determined quantitatively the amount of mechanical, and later electrical, energy expended in the propagation of heat energy, and established the mechanical equivalent of heat. This became the basis of the theory of energy conservation.

Joule was elected a Fellow of the Royal Society in 1850 and was awarded the Copley Medal in 1860.

Judas

A *judas* is someone who betrays a friend, a traitor. The term comes from the name of Christ's betrayer, Judas Iscariot.

In the English language, the word has come to be associated with betrayal or slyness of various kinds. A *judas kiss* denotes outward courtesy but cloaks deceit. A *judas slit* is the hole in a prison wall through which a guard can observe his prisoner. The *judas tree*, which grows in southern Europe, bears its flowers before its leaves; it is said to be the species of tree from which the traitor finally hanged himself. *Judas hair* is red, said to be the colour of the disciple's; the phrase is used by Shakespeare in *As You Like It*.

Juggernaut

Nowadays in the West, the word *juggernaut* is applied to any huge motor vehicle. In Hindu mythology Juggernaut (meaning in Sanskrit 'Lord of the World') is the name of a great idol to the god Vishnu whose temple is located at Puri in Orissa. The chief annual festival (Rathayatra) held to celebrate the god is commonly known as the 'car festival' and is held in June/July; during it the statue is dragged along the road in a car 35 feet square and 45 feet in height. The car has sixteen wheels, each 7 feet in diameter. The journey takes several days and involves thousands of pilgrims, stories being told of fanatics even throwing themselves under the wheels of the car.

Jumbo

Jumbo – the name has been associated with anything of giant proportions, including the world's largest aircraft, and is the affectionate generic slang word for all elephants – was the given name of one particular elephant. Even among elephants Jumbo was something of a giant, standing 10 feet 9 inches at the shoulder and weighing six and a half tons. He resided in London Zoo for seventeen years, sustained by a daily ration of 200 pounds of hay, five pails of water and a quart of whisky.

In 1882, in a moment of financial necessity, Jumbo was sold to Phineas T. Barnum's circus, the Greatest Show on Earth, and shipped to America. The British public protested loudly and even Queen Victoria added her voice to demands that Jumbo, considered a national treasure, should remain in the country. But to no avail. The crossing took fifteen days; Jumbo survived by drinking enormous quantities of beer. During his three and a half years with the circus in America it was estimated that a million children rode on his back. In 1885 Jumbo was struck down and killed by a freight train; when his bones were examined they revealed that he was still not fully grown. Barnum stuffed his carcass and exhibited it in the Barnum Hall, Tufts University, where it was finally destroyed by fire in 1975. Jumbo's skeleton was sent to the Smithsonian Institute in Washington DC where it remains.

The name Jumbo itself is believed to derive either from 'mumbo-jumbo' or the Swahili word *jumbe*, meaning a chief.

Kit Kat

Originally the name *kit kat* (or *kit cat*) was given to portraits usually painted on a canvas measuring 28 by 36 inches, i.e. less than half length but including hands. The term originated from the Whig club founded in 1703 by the publisher Jacob Tonson. At one time it met at the house of a pastrycook called Christopher (or Kit) Cat, in Shire Lane, London, where the law courts now stand. Originally there were thirty-nine members, all favourable to the succession of the house of Hanover and including such eminent names as Walpole, Addison, Steele, Congreve and Vanbrugh. Sir Godfrey Kneller, himself a member, agreed to paint the portraits of the club's members. Later the club grew considerably and became known as the Kit Cat Club. Kneller's portraits, forty-two in all, now hang in the National Portrait Gallery, London.

The name soon became associated with food, one of Cat's specialities being mutton pies which were regularly eaten at club gatherings. The Kit-Kat chocolate bar owes its name to the club, which was disbanded *c.* 1720.

Leotard

The stretchy one-piece suit worn by dancers, acrobats, yoga and keep-fit devotees owes its name and existence to the unofficial patron of all gymnasts, Jules Leotard (1842–70).

Leotard was the most famous of all nineteenth-century French acrobats, performing in many countries including the UK. Amongst his other giddy claims to fame, he perfected the first aerial somersault. In his memoirs he wrote: 'Do you want to be adored by the ladies? A trapeze is not required, but instead of draping yourself in unflattering clothes, invented by ladies, and which give us the air of ridiculous mannikins, put on more natural garb, which does not hide your best features.' What else but the costume he himself wore at performances – the leotard?

Leotard died of smallpox at the early age of twenty-eight.

Lindy Hop

A type of jitterbug dance originating in the Harlem district of New York. This dance, which later developed many local variants of tap steps, twosteps, etc., commemorates the dramatic solo crossing of the Atlantic from Long Island to Paris in 1927 by the American aviator Captain Charles Lindbergh, flying a single-engined Ryan monoplane 'Spirit of St Louis'. A *hop* is slang for both a dance (*at the hop*) and a short aeroplane flight.

Linnaean

Carl von Linne, otherwise known as Linnaeus (1707–78), is regarded as the founder of modern botany because of his development of a botanical classification system known as Linnaean classification.

The son of a clergyman, Linne was born in southern Sweden, and as a boy was so keen on flowers that he was nicknamed 'the little botanist'. After studying at Lund and Uppsala, he was eventually appointed professor of botany at Uppsala University in 1741. He explored Swedish Lapland and produced his first major work, *Flora Lapponica* (1737). Linnaeus's system was first introduced in his book *Species plantarum* (1753) and was quickly adopted. He later applied his theories to classifying the animal and vegetable kingdom.

Loganberry

A bramble shrub bearing edible purplish-red fruit similar to a blackberry, named after the American lawyer James H. Logan (1841–1928). Born in Indiana, Logan taught for a period and then moved westwards, driving an ox team for the Overland Telegraph Company. When he reached California, he studied law, was admitted to the bar in 1865, served as district attorney and later as judge of the superior court of Santa Cruz County between 1880 and 1892, when he retired.

Logan's hobby was horticulture, and in 1880 he started an experimental fruit and vegetable garden. He planted a row of wild California blackberries between a row of Texas early blackberries and red Antwerp raspberries. A year later he planted the second generation seedlings, which yielded two distinct fruits – a different tasting blackberry and another plant which more resembled a raspberry. The latter had a distinctive and delightful flavour. Thus it was that the loganberry was born.

The first fruit was produced in 1881 and it was introduced into Europe *c*. 1897.

Lucy Stoner

A *Lucy Stoner* is an American colloquialism for a woman who retains her maiden name in marriage. Lucy Stoner was an American suffragette (1818–93), who refused to change her name when she married a Mr Blackwell.

Lush

This term for a drunkard, especially used to describe a woman who is in the habit of having too much to drink, has curious eponymous origins.

Although the word was first popularized in the United States, its roots lie in England. In the nineteenth century, *lush* was a slang term for beer, after the name of an actors' drinking club called the City of Lushington, which was associated with the Harp Tavern in Great Russell Street, London. Dr Thomas Lushington (1590–1661), was a chaplain who was very fond of his tipple, and the drinking club may have derived its name from his. A favourite drinking companion was Bishop Richard Corbet, and whenever they met to embark on a drinking session they would commence with the words, 'Here's to thee, Corbet,' and 'Here's to thee, Lushington.'

Lynch

Many dictionaries still attribute the origins of *lynch*, to denote a mob killing of a supposed offender, usually by hanging, to Charles Lynch (1736–96), a Quaker from Virginia, who was a pacifist, although he was a colonel by the end of the American Civil War. He would toss people into gaol on illegal grounds but there is no evidence that he took this rough justice any further. However, the most likely originator of the word was a contemporary of Charles, William Lynch, who first turns up in an 1836 newspaper editorial written by Edgar Allan Poe. Poe discusses the law on lynching and writes 'The law, so called, originated in 1780, in Pittsylvania, Va. Col. William Lynch, of that county, is its author.'

Poe goes on to describe how Lynch took the law into his own hands to punish a group of ruffians who were robbing and vandalizing property. He formed a vigilante band and charged each member to uphold the law and to 'inflict such corporeal punishment on him or them, as to us shall seem adequate to the crime committed. . . .'

In 1788 Lynch became a member of the Virginia House of Delegates. Ten years later he moved to South Carolina where he spent the rest of his life. Little would be known about Lynch were it not for the diaries of Andrew Ellicot, a surveyor, who visited him in 1811. He recorded that: 'William Lynch was the author of the Lynch Laws so well known and so frequently carried into effect some years ago in the southern states. . . . The Lynch men associated for the purpose of punishing crimes in a summary way without the tedious and technical forms of our court justice. . . . Mr Lynch informed me that he had never in any case given a note for the punishment of death; some however he acknowledged had been actually hanged though not in the common way; a horse, in part, became the executioner; the manner was this – the person who it was supposed ought to suffer death was placed on a horse with his hands tied behind him and a rope about his neck which was fastened to the limb of a tree over his head. In this situation the person was left and when the horse in pursuit of food or any other cause moved from his position the unfortunate person was left suspended by the neck – this was called aiding the civil authority.'

Another possible derivation is from James Lynch Fitz-Stephens, the mayor of Galway, who hanged his own son in 1793 on a charge of murder, the execution being carried out from a window in his own house.

Lynching was quite common in the USA from the end of the Civil War up to the 1930s, especially for Negroes. Between 1840 and 1860 alone 300 people were hanged or burned by lynch law.

Macadam

Most roads are now *macadamized*; the process involves
compacting together layers of small hard stones, nowadays
with tar added. In McAdam's system, first stated in print in
his *Practical Essay on the Scientific Repair and Preservation of
Roads* (1819), the small stones were originally compacted by
the weight of traffic, but later rollers were introduced and
the addition of tar came with the registration of the name
Tarmac in the USA in 1903.

John McAdam (1756–1836) was born in Scotland. As a
child he made miniature roads – painstakingly laid out,
with tiny stones and perfect drains – in his back garden. At
the age of fourteen he was sent to America to work in his
uncle's business in New York and he returned in 1783 with
a comfortable fortune. McAdam revived his childhood
interest in roads, and his enthusiastic lobbying resulted in a
commission to construct 150 miles of road around Bristol;
these were completed in 1816.

McAdam's invention arose out of necessity. At the
beginning of the nineteenth century British roads needed
attention – at best they were rubble causeways and often
merely muddy tracks. To prevent flooding, the main roads
were built up so high that two vehicles could seldom pass
each other.

The new roads were a success and in 1827 McAdam was
made surveyor general of all metropolitan roads in the UK.
People came from miles around to see and drive along them.
Commissions for work flooded in. First Charing Cross, the
Quadrant to Piccadilly, then Regent Street and Bond
Street, and finally most of London's central muddy arteries
were converted into smooth macadamized roads.

Although his life and future were now secured, not
everyone appreciated McAdam. A cartoon of the day shows
him, wearing a kilt, straddling the intersection of the Great
North Road and the Great West Road. The caption reads:
'Mock-Adam-Izing – the Colossus of Roads'. Soon, though,
even the sceptical were won over and McAdam became a
part of the language within his lifetime. In *Festus*, Thomas
Bailey's Lucifer says:

> *I should like to Macadamize the world*
> *The Road to Hell wants mending!*

And Thomas Hood even wrote an 'Ode to Mr M'Adam'.

Mach number

The name given to the expression of the ratio of flight speed to the speed of sound at sea level; thus, Mach 1 = 750 m.p.h. (the speed of sound).

The Austrian physicist and philosopher Ernst Mach was born in Moravia in 1838. He held successive chairs at three European universities: Grax (mathematics), Prague (physics) and Vienna (philosophy of inductive sciences). As well as formulating the Mach number, he gave his name to the Mach angle – the angle between the axis of a projectile and the envelope of the pressure waves which it produces. He had a seminal influence on the important Vienna circle of logical positivists.

Machiavellian

Characterizing an unscrupulous lust for power.

Niccolo Machiavelli (1469–1527) was born in Florence of a distinguished family. From 1498 until 1512 he held the post of secretary and second chancellor of the Florentine republic and was strongly opposed to the return to power of the Medici family. As a result, when they did return in 1512, he was imprisoned and tortured to extract a confession of conspiracy against the family. He denied the charge and was finally pardoned, although obliged to withdraw from public life.

During his period of home imprisonment, he devoted himself to writing, including drama, and completed his great work, *The Prince*, for which he is best remembered today. In the book, completed in 1514, Machiavelli studies power – how to get it and, most important, how to keep it. Rulers of the past are used as examples and Cesare Borgia, although disliked by Machiavelli, is cited as the model prince for his ability to seize and hold the reins of government.

Machiavelli was a staunch realist; he maintained that the retention of power is more important than being loved and respected, and that although virtue may be commendable, it is not practical. In short, his thesis states that the end justifies any means. In the hope that he might make up his differences with the family, he dedicated the book to Lorenzo de' Medici, but to no avail.

However, on Lorenzo's death, Machiavelli emerged again into the public eye and, in 1519, Pope Leo X (Giovanni de' Medici) commissioned him to write a report on the reform of Florence; this completed, he went on to work in the diplomatic service. He died in 1527.

Mackintosh

Charles Macintosh (1766–1843), a Glaswegian clerk turned chemist, did not invent the *mackintosh*, which originally was not the weatherproof garment but a type of rubberized cloth.

James Symes (1799–1870), who later became a surgeon, invented the process at the age of seventeen, but it was patented by Macintosh in 1823. A keen amateur chemist Macintosh soon became dissatisfied with life as a clerk and began manufacturing sal ammoniac. In 1797 he started Scotland's first alum plant and became well known for inventing a number of important chemical processes. Having refined Symes's method for producing waterproof cloth by cementing two pieces of fabric together with india rubber dissolved in naptha, Macintosh began producing a material that was suitable not only for raincoats but for life preservers, diving suits and hot-water bottles. Its usefulness was soon appreciated.

Captain William Parry, the explorer, ordered a supply of waterproof canvas bags, air beds and pillows for his Arctic expedition. He later wrote, 'Just before halting at 6 a.m. on the 5th July 1827, the ice at the margin of the flow broke while the men were handling provisions out of the boats; and we narrowly escaped the loss of a bag of cocoa, which fell overboard, but fortunately . . . this bag, being made out of Macintosh's waterproof canvas, did not suffer the slightest injury.'

The first raincoat made of macintosh cloth – the first *mac* – appeared in 1830.

Mae West

The obvious charms of the great American film star Mae West, who is reported to have admitted that she did 'all her best work in bed', lent their name to the airman's pneumatic lifejacket. When inflated, it was said to give the wearer a generous bosom like Mae's own. The name was first given to the lifejacket by RAF personnel in the Second World War. This honour led Mae West to say, 'I've been in *Who's Who* and I know what's what, but it's the first time I ever made the dictionary.'

An army tank with two turrets was also called a *Mae West*.

Major Mitchell

To Major Mitchell is a quaint Australian expression which describes someone travelling a zigzag course across country. It derives from Major Sir Thomas Mitchell (1792–1855), who was Surveyor General to the state of New South Wales in 1828. He set out to explore the Australian interior and in particular to see if the Darling and Murray rivers shared a common source, which was in fact the case. While on his journey he became wildly lost and covered many unnecessary miles to conduct his explorations – hence today's slang term.

A *Major Mitchell* is also a variety of cockatoo.

Malapropism

Mrs Malaprop is a favourite eccentric in English literature whose name has now become associated with linguistic blunders.

Mrs Malaprop – *mal à propos* is a French expression meaning inappropriate or out of place – is a character in *The Rivals* (1775), the comedy by Richard Brinsley Sheridan (1751–1816). Full of romantic intrigue and muddle, *The Rivals* is essentially a farce on the etiquette demanded in those days, and provides plenty of scope for Mrs Malaprop to utter such lines as 'headstrong as an allegory [alligator] on the banks of the Nile'.

Malapropisms are usually made by people trying to impress others with their command of language and in the process only proving their inadequacy. George Eliot wrote, 'Mr Lewis is sending what a malapropian friend once described as a missile to Sara.' Other examples from *The Rivals* include: 'He is the very pineapple of politeness' and 'a supercilious knowledge in accounts . . . and something of the contagious countries'.

This humourous device was not invented by Sheridan; Shakespeare puts similar topsy-turvy phrases in the mouth of Dogberry in *Much Ado About Nothing*, and in *Humphrey Clinker* (1771) Smollett introduces a character called Winifred Jenkins who has a tendency towards inappropriate language. But it is Sheridan's Mrs Malaprop who has won immortality.

Malley's cow
This Australian expression can be used of anyone who disappears without leaving a trace. The term originated when one Malley, who was responsible for looking after a cow during a cattle muster, failed to notice that it had disappeared. When questioned as to what happened, Malley scratched his head and replied, 'She's a goner.'

Marconigram
A *marconigram* was the original form of radiogram or wireless telegram. The Marchese Guglielmo Marconi was the inventor of wireless telegraphy. Marconi was born in Bologna in 1874, the son of an Italian nobleman and an Irish woman. He was the first person to send a signal across the Atlantic, in 1901. In 1909 he shared the Nobel Prize for his contributions to physics. He was also active in Italian politics and was president of the Italian Royal Academy in 1930. He died in 1937.

Marmalade
A kind of bitter jam, originally made from quinces but now generally of Seville oranges and containing pieces of peel, much favoured at breakfast in the UK. One colourful derivation for this word is from a story concerning Mary Queen of Scots. It is said that once, when she was ill, the only food that she could eat was this preserve, which henceforth was called Marie Malade (sick Mary). A more generally accepted origin is from the Portuguese *marmelada*, meaning quince conserve, from *marmelo*, meaning quince.

Martinet

A *martinet* is a punctilious, almost fanatical, disciplinarian.

Jean Martinet (who died in 1672) was a lieutenant colonel in the King's Regiment of Foot and inspector general of infantry in the reign of Louis XIV. He was instrumental in remodelling Louis's army into the first and best regular army in Europe. Earlier armies were composed largely of ill-disciplined mercenaries who supplied their own equipment. Martinet introduced strict, precise and tedious drilling for soldiers, thereby vastly improving their efficiency in battle. However, this gave him a reputation as a rigid disciplinarian. One of his methods of punishing soldiers was to whip them brutally with a cat-o'-nine-tails. The whip later became known as a *martinet*.

Ironically, Martinet was accidentally killed by his own men during the siege of Duisberg in 1672 while he was leading an infantry assault with such keenness that he found himself directly in line of the rear ranks' covering fire. A Swiss captain called Soury also died in the blast, an event which led some wit to note that Duisberg had cost the king only a martin and a mouse (French *souris*, mouse).

Originally the term *martinet* was common only in military circles, but its use widened later. Wycherly, in *The Plain Dealer* (1677), says, 'What, d'ye find fault with Martinet? . . . 'tis the best exercise in the World.'

Marzipan

A paste of almonds, sugar, etc., for covering cakes and often used to make shapes of fruits and figures as decoration or confectionery. It used to be eaten during the feast of St Mark (25 April) and derives its name from the Latin *Marci panis*, meaning Mark's bread.

Masochism

A form of sexual perversion in which one finds pleasure in abuse and cruelty from one's associates.

Leopold von Sacher-Masoch (1836–95) had a childhood full of tales of violence and torment. His wet nurse, Handsacha, would tell him gruesome stories of Ivan the Terrible, of Casimir III and others – all people whose lives were dominated by cruelty.

Leopold's father was a policeman in Austria, and also
enjoyed recounting tales of violence. Leopold was twelve
years old when he saw from his window bloody street
fighting during the 1848 Polish landowners' revolt against
the aristocracy. He began to compose little plays about
revolts, which he acted out in puppet theatres. His dreams
were haunted by executions and torture, dreams in which
he was always the victim.

Outwardly life progressed smoothly. He was a bright
pupil, and his family moved in high society in Graz.
Leopold became a lecturer in law at the age of twenty and at
twenty-one published *The Rebellion of Ghent under Charles V*.

At twenty-five he gave up his career and retreated to the
crazed world of his imagination, where his mother
transformed herself from a sweet gentle lady into a savage
bullying creature from the Carpathian mountains. He
found no joy in normal sexual intercourse and set out to find
himself a woman who would humiliate and hurt him. Pain,
he had discovered, was the necessary prelude to his
pleasure.

His first mistress was Anna Von Kottowitz, a beautiful
woman ten years his senior, who abandoned her children
and husband to live with him. She soon began to lose
interest in whips and birches, but Leopold would not leave
her until she had slept with another man. He loved her and
kept her in high style, writing feverishly to pay the bills.

When Anna left he signed a contract with his second
mistress, who, although he did not love her, was satisfactory
from a sexual viewpoint. In the contract he wrote, 'Herr
Leopold von Sacher-Masoch gives his word of honour to
Frau Pistor to become her slave and comply unreservedly
for six months with every one of her desires and commands.
. . . Frau Pistor, on her side, promises to wear furs as often
as possible, especially when she is in a cruel mood. . . .'
When they travelled, Frau Pistor would go first-class,
Leopold third. She deceived him with other men and was as
despotic and cruel as he desired. In short, the affair was a
success.

Leopold wrote his best-known book, *Venus in Furs*, during
this time and its detailed exposition of masochism made
him notorious. He fascinated women and was finally

ensnared by one who inveigled him into marriage. Wanda, who came from a humble family, pretended to enjoy inflicting pain, but what she really wanted was the grand name of Sacher-Masoch. Finally Leopold engineered her 'betrayal' of him and divorced her.

By this time he was a well-known and respected writer, although a figure of intrigue and gossip. His second marriage, to a young German woman, seems to have been more humane. His mind was failing and she finally had him committed to an asylum after he had made pathetic attempts to strangle her. Officially he died when he entered the asylum, and was publicly mourned. In fact he lived for another ten years, during which time the German psychiatrist Richard von Krafft-Ebing studied his works and immortalized his name by introducing the word *masochism* into the psychiatric dictionaries.

Maudlin

The term *maudlin*, meaning effusively and tearfully sentimental, and hence a stage of drunkenness, derives from Mary Magdalen. Modern biblical scholars argue that she was not a prostitute, as was once believed, rather that she repented of her profession. Some even say that the lonely lady from the fishing village of Magdala on the Sea of Galilee who devotedly followed Jesus and spent her later days ministering to his needs and those of his apostles was not the same woman who washed his feet in the house of Simon the Pharisee.

She is always portrayed as crying. Portraits by Titian, Veronese, Giotto, Georges de la Tour and many others show her weeping. It is said that she cries because when she saw the empty tomb, she thought not that Jesus had fulfilled his prophecy of rising from the dead, but that his body had been removed by grave-robbers.

Mauser rifle

The *Mauser* was the first practical working bolt-action repeating rifle. It was named after its inventors, Peter Paul Mauser (1838–1914) and Wilhelm Mauser (1834–82), sons of a German gunsmith. In 1867 they moved to Belgium where they set up a workshop in Liège. Two years was needed to perfect their idea for a bolt-action rifle, which they were able to sell in great quantities to the Prussian army. The brothers returned to Oberndorf in Germany and founded the enormous and hugely successful Mauser factory. The gun was first used in Germany in the 1880s and fired five rounds of ammunition from a charger. The design was so successful that versions of this weapon continued to be used by the German army until the end of the Second World War.

Mausoleum

This name for a large and elaborate tomb or monument derives from King Mausolus, the king of Caria in ancient Greece between 377 and 353 BC.

Before he died, Mausolus designed his own tomb and left instructions for its construction. It was, he insisted, to be grandiose, of white marble, over 100 feet high, and to include in its accompanying statuary figures of himself and of his wife.

When he died, his wife Artemisia arranged for the tomb to be constructed according to Mausolus's wishes at Halicarnassus. The result was magnificent and was immediately pronounced the seventh wonder of the world. It survived in good condition for many years but was destroyed by earthquakes in the twelfth century. Much of the remaining material was used to build the fortress of San Pietro in 1404. In 1846 Sir Charles Newton brought parts of the frieze and the two huge statues to England where they were placed in the British Museum.

Maverick

Today the term *maverick* can be applied to any wild and unconventional person, although the word originally referred to cattle which had gone astray or had no owner.

Samuel A. Maverick (1803–70) was a Texas cattle rancher who could not be bothered to brand his herd. His property covered 385,000 acres and some 400 of his cattle strayed from his ranch. When Maverick put out an alert for them, his neighbours rounded up the missing cattle but refused to hand them over as they bore no brand marks and therefore could not be proved absolutely to be Maverick's. His fury attracted such attention that the language found itself with a new word.

Later, the term *maverick* was applied in a political sense to describe a politician who does not toe the party line.

McCarthyism

A political witch-hunt.

Joseph Raymond McCarthy (1909–57), the American politician, was born in Wisconsin. After serving in the US Marines, he was elected to the Senate as a Republican in 1946. Between 1945 and 1950 McCarthy exploited the growing American unease arising from the trials for treason of Fuchs, Alger Hiss and Nunn May, and he was returned to the Senate with a huge majority at the subsequent election.

After Eisenhower's victory in 1948, McCarthy was appointed head of the powerful Permanent Subcommittee on Investigations, and he mercilessly hounded prominent Americans, especially Hollywood figures, writers and television personalities, charging them with Communist sympathies. People lost their jobs in this period, either because of suspicions directed against them or because they refused to give evidence against their friends.

McCarthy accused the State Department of harbouring 205 prominent Communists. This brought him great notoriety, but he was unable to substantiate the charge before a Senate Committee on Foreign Relations. Undaunted, he continued his activities, accusing the Truman administration of being 'soft on Communism' and the Democratic Party in general of being guilty of 'twenty years of treason'.

Army generals reacted strongly when they were accused and Ed Murrow exposed McCarthy on television in front of an audience of millions. At last, McCarthy having even been brazen enough to attack Eisenhower himself, the Senate felt he had gone far enough and in 1954 he was formally condemned.

McCoy

The phrase *the real McCoy*, indicating indisputable authenticity, has a highly disputable origin. According to Eric Partridge in *From Sanskrit to Brazil* (1952) the expression, originally 'the real MacKay', dates from the 1880s, where it was applied in Scotland to men and whisky of the highest quality. Connected with this is the theory that the phrase derives from the fact that there are two main branches to the MacKay clan. Because of this, there is constant dispute over who is the true head of the clan, the *real* MacKay. The phrase was transported along with the men and the whisky, to the USA, and there it stuck.

Others, however, claim that the term originated with the boxer Norman Selby (1873–1940), whose fighting name was Kid McCoy. They tell of a drunk who quarrelled with the champion, who did all he could to avoid a fight. Onlookers warned the drunk who the man he was provoking was, but he persisted. Finally McCoy had had enough and knocked his challenger out with a punch. When he came round, the drunk shook his head and ruefully admitted, 'You're right, that was the real McCoy.'

Mesmerize

To induce a hypnotic state.

Franz (or Friedrich) Anton Mesmer (1734–1815) was born near Constance in Germany and studied medicine at Vienna. He held doctorates in medicine, law and philosophy. He was a truly learned man in the Renaissance tradition, although many later came to view him as something of a dilettante and a bumbler.

Mesmer was fascinated by the planets and their influence on the human body and believed that the universe was filled with a magnetic fluid which permeated everything and conveyed the influence of the stars. He claimed to be able to control this power and, to prove it, constructed a series of iron rods. Patients would hold the rods and each others' hands whilst Mesmer waved a magnetic wand. Some people were cured, though on what scientific basis it is hard to fathom. News spread and people flocked to the powers of Mesmer's magnet.

However, despite the support of his patients, the

Austrian authorities forced him to leave Vienna and he arrived in Paris in 1778. Here, clad in purple robes and carrying his magnetic wand, he would hold group meetings. With dim lights and soft music, Mesmer would challenge a patient with a sudden question about his or her ailment. Tensions ran high and patients would finally break into twitching and screaming, the crisis that Mesmer believed to be part of the cure and the result of his personal power or 'animal magnetism'.

In 1784 Louis XVI appointed a committee to investigate this man whose fame had reached the proportions of religious mania. On the committee sat Dr Guillotin, Benjamin Franklin and Lavoisier, and their conclusion was that 'imagination with magnetism produces convulsions and that magnetism without imagination produces nothing'. This finally drove Mesmer from Paris. Vienna was still closed to him so he lived the rest of his life in obscurity in Switzerland. He died never realizing what he had stumbled on – the power of hypnotism and its use in healing, which was to be taken up and developed into its modern form by the British surgeon James Braid.

Mickey Finn

A *Mickey Finn* is a substance secretly slipped into someone's drink to render them unconscious. Mickey Finn was a Chicago bartender who worked in a downtown bar from *c*. 1896 to 1906. He was obviously an unscrupulous fellow, who would slip a potion (probably containing chloral hydrate) into his customers' drinks so they passed out. Mickey Finn and his boys would then rob them.

Mithridatize

The slow process of creating immunity against a poison by administering small quantities of a toxin or virus until sufficient antibodies have been built up is known as *mithridatizing*.

The word derives from the name of an ancient king, Mithridates VI (120–63BC), called the Great, who was king of Pontus, a district in Asia Minor bordering on the Black Sea. Mithridates was Rome's strongest oriental antagonist and at one time held sway over Asia Minor, much of Greece and all the islands of the Aegean except Rhodes. Modelling himself on Alexander in appearance, he engaged the Romans in three major wars, and was eventually defeated by Pompey at Nicopolis. Due to his constant fear of assassination, Mithridates had over the years administered small doses of poison to his own body, thereby making himself immune. However, on his defeat by Pompey, he sought to take his own life by poison. When this failed, he ordered a Gallic mercenary to kill him with his sword.

Molotov cocktail

A Molotov cocktail is a home-made hand grenade, usually in the form of a petrol bomb, which was named after the fiery Russian politician, Vyacheslav Mikhailovich Skriabin, known as Molotov ('the Hammer'), although not invented by him. It was first used by the Finns against Russian tanks in 1940 and was then developed in Britain as one of the weapons of the Home Guard. The device is simple to make and consists of a bottle containing inflammable, glutinous liquid, with a slow fuse protruding from the neck. The fuse is lit and the bottle hurled against the side of a tank, where it bursts into flames, spreading the burning liquid across the metal surface.

Molotov was a key figure in Russian politics in the first half of this century. He was born in 1890 and joined the Bolsheviks at the age of sixteen. After helping to found *Pravda* in 1912 with Stalin, his career in the Communist Party proceeded apace and he was chairman of the Council of People's Commissars (equivalent to premier) from 1930 to 1941, when he was succeeded by Stalin. During this time he became an internationally known figure and took on the additional post of Commissar for Foreign Affairs in 1939. His role led to the shaping of the non-aggression pact with Nazi Germany. After the Second World War he emerged as the champion of world Sovietism, but it was his attitudes that led to the prolongation of the Cold War and the division of Germany into two zones. He fell from grace in 1957 when Khrushchev referred to him as a saboteur of peace, accused him of policy failures, and finally sent him to Mongolia as ambassador. He was expelled from the party in 1964 and disappeared into obscurity.

Monkey wrench

A spanner or wrench with an adjustable jaw set at right
angles to the handle, probably the invention of Charles
Moncke, a London blacksmith. An alternative origin is that
the name derives from an American called Monk, *c.* 1856.

Morse Code

A telegraphic code in which letters are represented by
groups of dots and dashes.

Samuel Breese Morse (1791–1872) was born in
Charleston, Massachusetts, the son of a geographer and
clergyman. He graduated from Yale and then went to
England to study painting and design. On his return to New
York he became the founder and the first president of the
National Academy of Design (1826–45).

As a student, Morse had always been interested in
electricity; although he continued studying the Old
Masters, he devoted much of his time to designing
prototypes of his telegraph. Recognition was slow but, in
1843, financed by Congress, the first telegraph line came
into being between Baltimore and Washington. Following a
number of legal battles, Morse patented his famous code in
1854, and the system is still in use today.

Morse lived to see his system adopted by other countries,
many of which recognized him as a great inventor.
Napoleon III conferred substantial national honours on
Morse. He died in 1872 and a bronze statue was erected in
New York to his memory.

Mosey

This American slang word meaning to stroll, as in *to mosey
along*, stems from the name given to Jewish street vendors in
the USA who used to slouch under the weight of their loads.
A general name applied to all Jews at one time was Moses.

Mudd

Your name is mud or *Here's mud in your eye* – both the insult and
the toast have a curious common origin.

John Wilkes Booth, the assassin of Abraham Lincoln
(1809–65), bungled his escape after committing the crime.
His spurs caught in the flags decorating the President's·

theatre box and he fell heavily, breaking his leg in the
process. Despite this, Booth escaped and sought treatment
for his injury from Dr Samuel Mudd (1833–83), a country
doctor who did then not know of the President's
assassination.

The following day Mudd and his wife learned about the
assassination and grew suspicious. They notified the
authorities, who did not believe Mudd's innocence,
convicted him on a charge of conspiracy and sentenced him
to life imprisonment. The American people were so
incensed and furious about the assassination that they
would not listen to Mudd's pleas and he lived out his life in
jail. It became fashionable to associate the name Mudd
with anything connected with the assassination.

Mudd was officially pardoned in 1869 by President
Andrew Johnson.

Namby-pamby

Namby-pamby – the derisive adjective used to describe
anyone who is insipid or weakly sentimental – comes from
the nickname given to the poet Ambrose Philips
(1674–1749). Originally it was restricted to writers who
displayed such traits as Philips, but in recent times its
application has widened.

Ambrose Philips was a minor poet, a writer of pretty but
vapid pastoral verse. He was commissioned to compose
some lines for the children of Lord Carteret, and the result
inspired Henry Carey, the author, dramatist and ballad
writer who composed 'Sally in our Alley', to dub Philips
Namby Pamby. The term was eagerly seized upon by Pope,
who had quarrelled with Philips and was always pleased to
insult him. Dr Johnson described the quarrel between the
two authors as a 'perpetual reciprocation of malevolence'.
They argued principally about the relative merits of their
work.

Nap

The card game *nap* was named after Napoleon Boneparte
(1769–1821). In the game each player receives five cards
and calls in advance the number of tricks he expects to

make. The one who calls five is said to be *going nap*; if he succeeds then he has *made his nap*. The game was particularly popular in the nineteenth century.

Negus

Sweet wine, usually port or sherry, with hot water, lemon and spices added, is commonly known as *negus*. The name derives from its inventor – or maybe the name was attributed to him because he enjoyed the tipple so much – Francis Negus (d. 1732).

A modern version of negus consists of the following:

> *A bottle of sherry*
> *1 quart of boiling water*
> *1 lemon*
> *1 measure of brandy*
> *nutmeg*
> *sugar*

Warm the sherry gently in a saucepan, add the sliced lemon and pour in the boiling water. Add a little nutmeg and sugar to taste; finally add the brandy. Makes about twelve glasses.

Nicotine

The chemical formula for nicotine is $C_{10}H_{14}N_2$ and in its unadulterated form it is a poisonous alkaloid. We know it better as the soothing component of tobacco.

The word *nicotine* derives from Jean Nicot, Sieur de Villemain, a French diplomat and scholar who was born at Nîmes in 1530. As ambassador to Portugal in 1560, Nicot was introduced to tobacco in Lisbon and in the following year he returned to Paris with a cargo of the plant, which was subsequently named *Nicotiana* in his honour. Sir Walter Raleigh introduced tobacco into England shortly afterwards.

Tobacco was soon highly fashionable in Europe, but after the initial enthusiasm came a period of persecution. The Bishop of Granada was deeply offended because his flock sneezed all the way through his sermon. A theological dispute arose. Did a pinch of snuff constitute breaking a fast? Pope Innocent X disapproved of the substance so strongly that he excommunicated all tobacco users. Outside France the furore raged; the Russian tsar ordered snuff-sniffers' noses to be cut off. The Persian shah, Sifi, impaled users.

In the end, commerce triumphed over morality and the French discovered that a simple state tax of two francs per 100 pounds of tobacco brought in roughly one million francs a year. Tobacco was back in favour.

Nosey parker

This expression for someone who is continually curious about the affairs of others derives from a sixteenth-century Archbishop of Canterbury, Dr Matthew Parker (1504–75).

Parker began his career as a Fellow of Corpus Christi College, Cambridge. Having taken holy orders in 1527, he became chaplain to Anne Boleyn and later to Henry VIII. He was canon of Ely in 1541 and master of Corpus Christi, in 1544, but resigned under Mary in 1553. With the accession of Elizabeth I he bacame Dean of Lincoln (1552) and then Archbishop of Canterbury (1559). A Protestant, he was fanatically religious and soon acquired a reputation for continually scrutinizing all matters of Church business. In 1568, he originated a new translation of the Bible (known as the Bishops' Bible, superseded by the King James version in 1611), as well as editing several religious works. Catholics did not like either Parker or the fact that there was a Protestant Archbishop. The scandalous fable that his consecration took place informally in an inn called the Nag's Head originated in Catholic circles and was touted as a reason for questioning the sincerity of his faith.

Oakes's oath

Oakes's oath is an Australian expression to describe a testimony that, although sworn, should not be taken seriously. A man called Oakes was produced in court as a witness in a trial involving a large number of stolen cattle. Asked if he could identify a pair of horns that were said to have once belonged to one of the stolen beasts, Oakes scratched his head and said, 'I'll chance it; Yes.'

Ohm

The unit of resistance to the flow of electricity through a conductor. Ohm's Law, propounded in 1843, states that electromotive force (measured in volts) = current (in amps) × resistance (in ohms).

Georg Simon Ohm was born in Germany in 1787. By the age of twenty-two, Ohm had a doctorate in physics, and he prepared to support himself by teaching. His life was hard, and repeated letters to the King of Bavaria asking for financial support while he pursued his research met with no success. It took the publication of his first book to push Ohm into the public eye. He mailed signed copies to all the monarchs of Europe and the King of Prussia decided to sponsor the young scientist. He was invited by Friedrich Wilhelm to teach at the Royal Konsistorium in Cologne where he developed his theory of electrical circuits. Ohm received the Royal Society's Copley Medal in 1841 and was appointed professor of physics at Munich Univeristy in 1849.

Ohm died in 1854. His contribution to science was officially recognized in 1893 when the International Electrical Congress met to assign names to the various electrical units of measure. Ohm was duly honoured.

Oscar

The name given to the golden statuettes awarded annually for 'outstanding performance in the various fields of the motion picture industry'.

When the idea of an award was first introduced in Hollywood in 1927, the year the Motion Picture Academy was founded, the statuettes were nameless. And so they remained for four years.

In 1931 Mrs Margaret Herrick, later to become secretary of the Academy, saw for the first time the small golden figure. She wryly observed that the statue 'reminds me of my Uncle Oscar'. As chance would have it, a newspaper columnist with little copy to file that day overheard her remark. 'Employees,' he wrote, 'have affectionately dubbed their famous statuette "Oscar".'

Mrs Herrick's 'uncle' was in fact her second cousin, Oscar Pierce, son of a wealthy western pioneer family, who had formerly lived in Texas. His main concerns were wheat and fruit; whether he was interested in the cinema is not known.

The statuette, which was originally designed for the Academy by George Stanley, a Los Angeles sculptor, is 10 inches high and weighs 7 pounds. The inside is bronze and the exterior gold plate.

Palladian

An architectural style characterized by symmetry and monumentality and using classical forms, based on the work of the Roman architect Vitruvius and popularized in the sixteenth century by Andrea Palladio.

Born Andrea di Pietro in Vicenza in 1508, Palladio began life as a stonemason and sculptor before receiving the patronage of the scholarly poet Trissimo, who also rechristened him, naming him after an angel in one of his own poems who is portrayed as explaining the divine significance of geometrical forms in architecture.

Palladio learned his trade quickly and after a period of study and travel, began to develop a style of his own based on the work of the first-century Roman architect Vitruvius. Palladio was described as 'the Raphael of architects' and most of his greatest works, including the Villa Rotunda at Vicenza and S. Giorgio Maggiore in Venice, are situated in the vicinity of his home town. However, his greatest influence was on seventeenth- and eighteenth-century European architecture, especially on Inigo Jones (1573–1652), who introduced the style to Britain. A noted example of Jones's work is the Banqueting Hall in Whitehall.

Pander

To pander to is to minister to the baser passions or evil designs of others. The word derives originally from Homer's *Iliad*. In this great epic of the Trojan war, Pandarus is an archer who wounds Menelaus, Helen of Troy's husband, thereby breaking the truce between the Greeks and the Trojans.

The modern sense of *pander* comes from the fictionalized romances taken from Homer by Boccaccio (*Filostrato*),

Chaucer ('Troylus and Cryseyde'), Shakespeare (*Troilus and Cressida*) and others. In these versions Pandarus (or Pander) is seen as the go-between for the two lovers, Troilus, son of Priam, king of Troy, and Cressida, daughter of a priest who has fled Troy and left her behind. As Pandarus says: 'If ever you prove false one to another, since I have taken such pains to bring you together, let all pitiful goers-between be called to the world's end after my name; call them all Pandars' (*Troilus and Cressida* III, ii, 195–200).

Panic

The word for the sudden sensation of fright derives from Pan, the ancient Greek god of flocks and fertility, called Faunus by the Romans. In some accounts he is the son of Hermes and Penelope. At his birth he startled everyone, especially his mother, as he was born covered in hair and had the feet, legs, ears and horns of a goat. His father swiftly bore him away to Olympus to see what could be done, but the gods, instead of being alarmed, were delighted.

Greek shepherds regard Pan as their special protector; he is also associated with the patronage of fishing and bee-keeping. He was renowned for his great love of music, which he played on the famous pipes of Pan.

Pan was a mischievous creature and loved to appear and disappear suddenly, startling his audiences and making men stampede like cattle. It was he who was supposed to have caused the *panic* among the Persians at Marathon. Pan was also fond of making weird noises at night, and it is from these two aspects of the mythological figure that we derive the modern word *panic*. Strictly speaking, we should use an expanded expression and talk of people being seized by *panic fear*.

Pantaloons

Pantaloons, from which are derived the modern words *pants*, *underpants*, etc., were originally the baggy trousers worn by a character in the Italian *commedia dell'arte*. Pantaloon is the lecherous parent or guardian who is outwitted by the young lovers in the comedy. He is normally portrayed as a foolish old man wearing spectacles, slippers and baggy trousers.

His face is covered by a half-mask with a long, sharp, hooked nose and he wears a flat cap.

Pantaloon's own name comes from that of San Pantaleone, a fourth-century physician who became the patron saint of physicians and was adopted as the favourite saint of Venice. Thus the Venetians themselves are also represented by this character in the *commedia dell'arte*.

Parkinson's Law

Parkinson's law states that 'Work expands so as to fill the time available for its completion,' with the obvious corollary, 'Subordinates multiply at a fixed rate regardless of the amount of work produced.' In 1958, an English academic, Cyril Northcote Parkinson, published a humorous study of public and business administration called *Parkinson's Law or the Pursuit of Progress* and was launched overnight from relative obscurity to fame.

Parkinson's law was intended to be semi-serious, semi-satiric, but its basic truths are all too obvious and pinpoint some of the main reason for hopeless bureaucratic inefficiency and time-wasting.

Pasteurize

The discovery of the pasteurization process was a major scientific breakthrough. The process destroys undesirable organisms and limits the inevitable process of fermentation in milk, beer or other liquids, by sterilization at high temperatures.

Louis Pasteur was born in 1822, the son of a tanner. His first great love in life was painting, but this passion was soon superseded by a fascination with science. He entered the *Ecole Normale* in 1843 to study chemistry and later joined the faculty of science at the lycée at Dijon where he rose to the rank of professor. From Dijon he went to Strasbourg as professor of chemistry and married the rector's daughter, Marie Laurent, who was to become a devoted fellow worker and researcher. In 1854, aged only thirty-two, he accepted the position of professor of chemistry and dean of the science faculty of the University of Lille. It was at about this time that Pasteur, observing moulds growing on sour milk, hit on the idea that fermentation, rather than being spontaneous as previously held, was in fact due to micro-organisms carried in the air. To prove this, he tested sterile solutions which were only exposed to heated air and found that fermentation did not take place.

Thus was born the process of *pasteurization*, which, applied to milk, prevented such infectious diseases as Malta fever (brucellosis) and bovine tuberculosis, and is said to have saved France more money in wine that would otherwise have been ruined than the reparations claimed by Germany after the Franco-Prussian War of 1870.

Pasteur also found a vaccine for chicken cholera, and for anthrax, and his research on rabies led to the saving, in 1885, of a boy's life. Nine-year-old Joseph Meister had been bitten by a rabid dog and without treatment was certain to die. Sixty hours after the bite, Pasteur began administering the attenuated virus through the boy's abdomen. Once, sometimes twice a day, he gave the injections, and Joseph lived.

Louis Pasteur founded the Institut Pasteur in 1888 and continued working until his death in 1895. Of his life he said, 'I would feel that I had been stealing if I were to spend a single day without working.'

Pavlova

Anna Pavlova (1881–1931), the great Russian ballet dancer, was revered throughout the world. Born in St Petersburg the daughter of a soldier and a laundress, she graduated from the St Petersburg Theatrical School in 1899 and became prima ballerina of the Mariinski Theatre in 1906. She left four years later and toured with her own company. Perhaps her most famous role was as Giselle in Adam's ballet of the same name, and the solo *The Dying Swan* (1907), created for her by the choreographer Michel Fokine with music by Saint-Saëns.

To mark her performances in Australia and New Zealand, chefs there popularized a dish consisting of a meringue filled with tropical fruit and covered in cream. They called it a *pavlova*.

Pavlovian reaction
Ivan Petrovich Pavlov is one of the few physiologists whose
name has become a household word. He was born the son of
a priest in Ryazan near Moscow in 1849. His original
intention was to enter the priesthood like his father, but
instead, in 1870, he went to St Petersburg University to
study science and physiology, graduating in 1883. From
there he travelled to Leipzig and Breslau where he studied
under Ludwig and Heidman. He subsequently returned to
St Petersburg and later held the chair of physiology at the
Military Medical Academy (1895). In 1904 he was
awarded the Nobel prize for his research into the digestive
process.

Pavlov's major contribution to science came about
through his studies of the digestive tract. He discovered that
the secretion of gastric juices can be stimulated in dogs
without food actually reaching the stomach. If, every time a
dog is given food, a bell is rung, eventually the dog's
digestive enzymes, controlled by the vagus nerve, will be
produced at the sound of the bell alone. This transference of
a response from one stimulus to another stimulus is known
as conditioning; in humans such processes can lead to
inappropriate or irrational behaviour, hence the term
pavlovian reaction.

Pavlov's discoveries have played an important part in
present-day behavioural psychology and in the treatment of
neuroses. He died in 1936.

Peach Melba
Ice-cream and fruit confection.

Dame Nellie Melba, who was born Helen Porter Mitchell
in Australia in 1861, became a world-famous prima donna.
After a successful debut in Brussels in 1887, she appeared at
Covent Garden in 1888 and captivated her English
audience, especially G. B. Shaw. An operatic soprano,
Nellie took her new surname from Melbourne, near her
birthplace.

At the zenith of her career, Dame Nellie (she was so
honoured in 1918), consulted the Ritz's famous chef
Escoffier over the menu for a dinner party she was planning.
For dessert, she wanted *pêches flambées* but Ritz insisted that

an ice would be preferable. Escoffier settled the dispute by creating a new dish which combined both peaches and ice together with a raspberry sauce and whipped cream – *pêches Melba*. Though the ice-cold dish had little in common with Dame Nellie's fiery personality, she was delighted with the confection. She retired in 1926 and died in 1931.

Thin slices of toast, baked in the oven until they are golden brown, are called Melba toast.

Peeping Tom

Today *peeping tom* is synonymous with voyeur.

The origin of the expression goes back to the story of Lady Godiva's famous ride through the streets of Coventry. Godiva was the wife of Leofric, Earl of Mercia and Lord of Coventry, one of Edward the Confessor's greatest noblemen. According to the story, in 1040 Leofric imposed a tax upon the people of Coventry, but agreed to rescind it if Godiva would ride naked through the streets of the town.

Godiva accepted the challenge but ordered the inhabitants to stay indoors and cover their windows. The orders were followed by all but one person, an inquisitive tailor. What happened to Tom after he dared to gaze on the naked body of his lord's lady is uncertain. Some say he was killed by irate, or jealous, townsfolk; others say he was struck blind.

Peter out, to

This phrase, meaning to fade away or to come to nothing, is purported to owe its origin to the actions of St Peter after the arrest of Jesus. As predicted, his faith wavered when it came to the test and three times before the cock crowed he denied knowing Jesus (Luke 22). Other sources attribute it to mid-nineteenth-century America where it was used to described streams or mining seams coming to an end. Some sources even claim it derives from the French *péter*, to fart.

Peter Principle

The *Peter principle* states that 'In every hierarchy, whether it be government or business, each employee tends to rise to his level of incompetence; every post tends to be filled by an employee incompetent enough to execute its duties.'

Parkinson's law (q.v.) began the vogue for humourous
semi-scientific analysis and this principle is a continuation
of his method. *The Peter Principle – Why Things Always Go
Wrong*, by Lawrence J. Peter and Raymond Hull, was
published in 1969.

Petersham

A ribbed or corded stiffener used for giving extra strength to
skirt waistbands; the textured ribbon used in hat bands,
etc., and a variety of overcoat.

Charles Stanhope, fourth Earl of Harrington
(1780–1851), became a colonel in the British army in 1814
and was one of the best-known figures during the Regency
and the reign of George IV. A great eccentric, he is said
never to have gone out of his house until 6 p.m. and his
entire equipage was invariably of a brownish hue. As well as
designing the overcoat and cloth named after him in his
office as Lord Petersham, the earl also invented a snuff
mixture.

Philippic

Philippic, a word denoting bitter invective, derives from the
bad feeling that existed in the fourth century BC between
Demosthenes and Philip II of Macedon (383–335 BC), the
father of Alexander the Great.

Philip was a brilliant but ruthless and unscrupulous
strategist, and Demosthenes spent fifteen years denouncing
his politics to the Athenians. His aim was to turn them
against their aggressive ruler and he finally succeeded;
Philip was eventually murdered by one of his own courtiers.

Later, Cicero's speeches against Antony were called
philippics and resulted in the orator's death in 43 BC.

Pinchbeck

A metallic alloy; now commonly used to describe a cheap
imitation or even a counterfeit. Originally the word
described a zinc-copper alloy developed by Christopher
Pinchbeck (1670–1732), a Fleet Street watch- and
toy-maker. The alloy looked remarkably like gold, but it
was a fraction of the price, being five parts copper and one
part zinc. It was at first a welcome innovation, enabling

jewellers to produce low-cost, expensive-looking jewellery, as well as watch-chains, buckles, etc., which the public eagerly bought. However, due to the inevitable deceptions practised by some jewellers, the term *pinchbeck* acquired unpleasant connotations, and by the mid-nineteenth century the word had come to mean, in general terms, anything that was a shoddy imitation, or a spurious and deliberate fake.

The modern enthusiast for Victoriana is rarely troubled by whether a metal object is gold or not, and pinchbeck settings for paste stones, often of excellent workmanship, have become collectors' items.

Pindaric

Pindaric verse is irregular and of various metres; such was the style of Pindar, the Greek poet.

Pindar was born in about 522 BC near Thebes; he was a musician and song-writer as well as poet. In his writing he gives advice and reproof as well as praise to his patrons; at the zenith of his career Pindar was composing odes commissioned by people from all parts of the Greek world, from Syracuse and Macedon as well as the free cities of Greece.

Though he is said to have been prolific, very few examples of his work survive today. The best known of these are four books of Epinician odes, celebrating victories won in the Olympic, Pythian, Nemean and Isthmian games. They show an intense admiration for the Greek spirit and physique – Pindar considered these to be direct gifts of the gods.

Several modern poets attempted to copy his style, beginning with Cowley in his fifteen *Pindaric Odes* (1656) and later including Gray in *The Bard*, Dryden in *Threnodia Augustalis* and Pope. Jonathan Swift also tried, but his efforts were greeted by the comment from Dryden, 'Cousin Swift, you will never be a poet.'

Pitman

The word *Pitman* used to be almost synonymous with shorthand, though these days there are so many shorthand systems that Pitman's has largely been relegated to a description of one in particular.

Sir Isaac Pitman was born in Trowbridge, Wiltshire, in 1813. By trade he was a schoolteacher, but when in 1837 he published his *Stenographic Sound Hand*, a manual outlining the principles of a new shorthand, he gave up teaching and devoted the rest of his life to developing and refining his system. However, the schoolmaster in him never quite died and Pitman's other great cause was to campaign for spelling reform and consistency. Pitman's system was phonetically based and used dots, dashes, strokes and curves to signify various sounds. He was knighted in 1894 and died at Bath three years later.

Pitman's wife Meri died in 1857. To demonstrate his interest in spelling reform, he wrote her the following epitaph:

> *In memori ov*
> *Meri Pitman*
> *weif ov Mr Eizak Pitman*
> *Fonetik Printer, ov this Site*
> *Deid 19 Agust 1857 edjed 64*
> *'Preper tu mit thei God'*
> EMOS *4, 12*

Platonic

Spiritual, as opposed to sexual, love. Plato, the great Athenian philosopher, pupil of Socrates and author of the *Republic*, lived between about 428 and 348 BC. To Plato we owe almost all our knowledge of Socrates, whose life and teachings were faithfully recorded in his many works.

Plato was originally called Aristocles, but the name Plato is said to have been bestowed on him by his gymnastics teacher in deference to the great width of his shoulders.

The popular terms *platonic love* and *platonic friendship* signify friendship between members of the opposite sex that is devoid of sexual attraction. This concept is first found in the *Symposium*, where Plato lauds not the sexless love of a man for a woman but rather Socrates' love for young men, which was entirely without sexual implications.

Many people have argued that platonic love between a

man and a woman is impossible and that sex rears its head
sooner or later. Samuel Richardson in *Pamela* wrote that he
was convinced that platonic love is platonic nonsense.

Plato himself says in the *Republic*, 'The more the pleasures
of the body fade away, the greater to me is the pleasure and
charm of conversation.'

Plimsoll
Safety line on a ship, indicating how much cargo a vessel
can safely carry.

Samuel Plimsoll, the person responsible for introducing
them, was born in Bristol in 1824. He began his career as a
Sheffield brewery clerk and later, after steady promotion,
he started his own coal-dealing business in London.

At about this time, Plimsoll began to take an active
interest in the merchant shipping service and the dangers it
was exposed to. Ships, he noted, were often overloaded and
undermanned – 'coffin ships', whose owners hoped that
they would sink so they could claim the probably inflated
insurance money.

He worked hard to accumulate some damning evidence
about these matters, and when he entered Parliament as the
Liberal Member for Derby in 1868, his first move was to try
to secure passage of a government bill that would guard
against such fraudulent practices. Unfortunately, he was
unsuccessful. He published a short treatise, *Our Seamen*
(1872), which created a profound impression on a hitherto
largely ignorant population and resulted in Plimsoll being
appointed to a royal commission; subsequently a bill was
introduced. Plimsoll thought the bill was inadequate, but
better than nothing.

On one occasion in the House of Commons, Plimsoll lost
his temper when Disraeli announced that the bill would be
dropped. Plimsoll suspected that Disraeli was defending
the interests of rich ship owners, who stood to lose money
with the introduction of these safety laws. However, the
majority of the Commons were behind him and the bill
eventually became the Merchant Shipping Act of 1876,
giving wide powers to the Board of Trade to enforce the
regulations. The foremost of these was that every merchant
ship must carry a 'maximum load line' – immediately

known as the Plimsoll line. This line must first be marked by the owner and then later be checked by an official from the Board of Trade.

The Plimsoll line proved invaluable and resulted in far fewer sunken ships and the saving of many lives. Plimsoll himself was a great hero of the seamen, who elected him president of the Sailors' and Firemen's Union. Until his death in 1898, Plimsoll continued to campaign for greater safety measures at sea, transferring his attentions to the terrible plight of cattle when shipped by boat, publishing another booklet, *Cattle Ships*, in 1890.

Plimsoll is also responsible for another word in the language. The rubber-soled canvas shoes that bear his name are believed to be so-called because the upper edge of the mudguard resembles the Plimsoll line on a ship.

Pompadour

A shade of purple and an elaborate, usually high, coiffure.

The Marquise de Pompadour (1721–64) was the fourth and most witty, unscrupulous and imaginative mistress of Louis XV of France; she was certainly the most famous. Born Jeanne Antoinette Poisson in Potis, of humble origin, she married C. G. Le Normant d'Etoiles but divorced him on meeting the King in 1745; she was created official mistress and established at Versailles. The estate of Pompadour was acquired for her, thus conferring the title of Marquise de Pompadour. For the next two decades she exerted a tremendous influence upon national and international politics and numbered amongst her personal friends Voltaire and Montesquieu.

The Marquise was a highly attractive woman and she left her name to a number of fashions, in particular the *pompadour hairstyle*, in which the hair is turned back from the forehead in a roll.

Pompadour is also a colour between claret and purple; the fifty-sixth Foot Regiment (now part of the Third Battalion Royal Anglian Regiment) were nicknamed *Pompadours* from their use of this colour in their uniforms. There is even a tropical South American bird with brilliant crimson-purple plumage named after her.

Praline

Almonds or nuts browned in boiling sugar, eaten alone or
pulverized and used as a flavouring in chocolates, etc. The
sweet was originally concocted by the chef of Field Marshal
César de Choiseul, Count Plessis-Praslin.

Pry

Prying denotes objectionable curiosity and Paul Pry was a
superinquisitive person. The word derives from an 1825
farce by John Poole (1786–1872), entitled *Paul Pry*. Pry
always made his entrance with the line, 'I hope I don't
interrupt.'

Pullman

A *pullman* is a luxury railway sleeper carriage. Named after
its designer George Pullman, the carriage is fitted out to be
a salon by day and to convert at night into a sleeping car.

George Pullman (1831–97) himself amply fulfilled the
true American dream. He started out life working in a shop
and died a multi-millionaire.

Born in New York, Pullman trained as a cabinet-maker,
and decided early in life that the sleeping cars of his time left
a lot to be desired. He therefore set to work to convert two
day coaches of the Chicago & Alton railroad into sleepers
providing individual sleeping sections, washrooms, oil
lamps – all the trappings of comfort. Pullman also invented
a system whereby an upper berth could be hinged to the
side of the car and thus folded away when not in use.

Pullman soon realized he was on to a winner, but he
needed capital. So he went West to dig for it, literally.
Although he purportedly failed to find a gold mine, he
returned to Chicago with $20,000 which he invested in
building, with his friend Ben Field, his first carriage named
Pioneer. Unfortunately it was too high for many existing
bridges, but the carriage was so successful that, one by one,
the railroads raised the level of their bridges. After
President Lincoln's death the funeral party travelled to the
burial ground in Pullman's Pioneer. Having patented his
folding upper berth in 1864, Pullman developed a lower
berth system involving the passenger seats hinged in a

special way to form a bed. This was patented in the
following year.

Pullman set out to create hotels on wheels – or as near as
he could manage, given the limited space – and was so
successful that in 1867 he formed the Pullman Palace Car
Company and went on to design the Pullman diner. In the
1870s the menus included sirloin steak (50 cents) and snipe
and quail (75 cents).

Pullman flourished to such a degree that one of the
factories he founded to make railway carriages developed
into a small town – needless to say called Pullman – situated
outside Chicago. Pullman was not a kind employer and his
workers finally went on strike for higher pay. Twelve men
were killed in the ensuing riots and though Pullman finally
got his way, his tactics for ever tainted his name.

Pyrrhic victory

A *pyrrhic victory* is one in which the victor's losses are as great
as those of the defeated. The word is derived from Pyrrhus
(319–272 BC), king of Epirus and kinsman to Alexander the
Great. A great schemer and planner, he set out to conquer
the whole of the Western world, beginning in 280 BC by
invading Italy.

After a long and bloody year, he defeated the Romans at
Asculum in Apulia, but he lost so many men in the process
that he is reported to have said that if there were any more
such victories, then 'Pyrrhus is undone'. After this
prolonged battle, Pyrrhus's fortunes rapidly waned. The
final note of irony is that he died in Argos after being fatally
struck on the head by a tile thrown by an irate woman.

Queensberry Rules

John Sholto Douglas, the Eighth Marquis of Queensberry
(1844–1900) was a keen boxing enthusiast who with the
help of the noted athlete, John Graham Chambers,
supervised the drawing-up of a code of rules for the sport.
The rules were devised in 1867 and they remained in effect
until 1929, when they were superseded by those issued by
the British Boxing Board of Control. Hitting below the
waist-belt was outlawed by the Queensberry rules.

Perhaps the Marquis's most notable aggressive act was the accusation that led to his prosecution for criminal libel by Oscar Wilde. Queensberry was acquitted.

Quisling

This generic word for a traitor was taken from the name of one of the great traitors of the Second World War. Vidkun Abraham Quisling, who was born in Norway in 1887, became his country's most sinister politician. After graduating from military academy in 1911, he worked for the League of Nations, entering politics as an ardent anti-communist in 1929. He was Defence Minister in the Norwegian government from 1931–33 but resigned and later formed the Nasjonal Samling (National Unity) party. From its inception this right-wing party was unpopular among Norwegians and never gained more than 2.2 per cent of the national vote. In fact, it did not even have a representative in the Parliament.

With the rise of Nazism in Germany, Quisling found favour with Hitler and visited him in 1939. When on the morning of 9 April 1940 German troops landed in Oslo and took over the communication systems, Norwegians listened with amazement to the voice of their former Defence Minister as he announced that the King and parliament had left the capital and that he would assume their duties; in short, he would make himself prime minister.

However, even with Hitler's support, Quisling was soon in trouble. By 15 April the country was in such a state of anger that a revolution seemed imminent. The Germans removed Quisling from public office, but not into total obscurity. He remained *in absentia* head of the Nasjonal Samling and on 1 February 1942 was returned to the premiership. He moved into a forty-six-roomed villa on an island near Oslo, had the walls reinforced, bunkers built and machine-guns installed. He ate from gold and silver dishes but was so fearful of being poisoned that all his food had to be tasted for him.

Quisling, although greatly disliked, remained in office until the end of the occupation, but when, on 15 May 1945, the Germans in Norway surrendered, he was arrested. At his trial, he pleaded not guilty to the charge of treason but

the overwhelming evidence against him secured his
conviction. He was shot by firing squad on 24 October
1945.

Rabelaisian
The *Oxford English Dictionary* defines *Rabelaisian* as
'pertaining to . . . Rabelais or his writings which are
distinguished by exuberance of imagination and language,
combined with extravagance and coarseness of humour and
satire'.

François Rabelais (*c.* 1490–1553), the great French
novelist, published his most famous work, *Gargantua and
Pantagruel*, in five volumes between the years 1532 and 1552.
Born near Chinon in the province of Touraine, he took holy
orders and joined the Franciscan friars of
Fontenay-le-Comte, but later switched allegiance and
became a Benedictine monk. From the cloisters, Rabelais
entered medical school and practised and lectured at Lyons
and elsewhere, earning great respect as a physician and as a
pioneer of humanism and enlightenment.

His work is characterized by brilliant scholarship, satire
and a grossness of humour. 'What harm in getting
knowledge even from a sot, a pot, a fool, a mitten or an old
slipper?' he asked rhetorically. But even his satirical wit
could not mask the nobility that lay beneath. Professor
Dowdem in his critique of Rabelais said, 'Below his
laughter lay wisdom; below his orgy of grossness lay a noble
ideality.'

Rabelais railed with enormous power against the
immorality of the religious orders, against the pedantry of
doctors, against ascetics, spoil sports, prigs and prudes and
the folly of kings. He lived and worked in an age of
intolerance, when criticism was considered nothing short of
blasphemy and heresy and often met with torture and
death.

In an introductory poem to *Gargantua and Pantagruel*,
Rabelais wrote:

> *One inch of joy surmounts of grief a span*
> *Because to laugh is proper to the man.*

Rachmanism

Unscrupulous behaviour by landlords. *Rachmanism* is one of the newer words to find its way into the English language and, as with so many eponyms, it became common currency when there was a need for a single word to describe an action.

Under the Rent Act of 1957, rents in England were controlled at an artificially low level in comparison with the value of the property, provided that the tenancy did not change hands. The act was passed as a measure of protection to tenants, who otherwise would be at the whim and fancy of owners who might choose to raise the rents whenever they wanted. Though this law was passed with good intentions, it soon led to unscrupulous practices by some property owners, who would harass tenants in order to regain possession of a house or flat and then re-let at a substantially higher rent.

Peter Rachman, a Polish immigrant (1920–62), was just such a landlord. His beat was the Paddington area and his merciless activities were soon noted. Other landlords found guilty of such practices were soon dubbed *Rachmans* and *Rachmanism* became synonymous with exploitation of tenants.

Raglan

Raglan sleeves on coats and cardigans are not joined to the garment on the shoulder, but continue sloping from the bottom of the armhole up to the neck. A coat with sleeves of this sort was first worn by Fitzroy Somerset, Lord Raglan (1788–1855), the British commander-in-chief in the Crimean War, who lost his right arm, which was amputated without anaesthetic, after Waterloo. However, there seems to be no connection between his amputation and his choice of sleeve design.

Richter Scale

A scale for measuring the intensity of earthquakes. Invented by Charles Francis Richter (born 1900), professor of seismology at the California Institute of Technology, this device was developed in association with the German Dr

Bruno Gutenberg (1889–1960) and is sometimes known as the Gutenberg–Richter Scale.

Rickets

A disease affecting children caused by defective nutrition (especially a lack of vitamin D) and affecting bones, resulting in bow legs, spinal curvature, etc. According to John Aubrey's *Brief Lives* (1813), it is named after a Dr Ricketts of Newbury, 'a Practicioner in Physick', who became so adept at curing children with 'swoln heads and small legges' that the disease was called after him; 'and now 'tis good sport to see how they vex their Lexicons, and fetch it from the Greek ραχίς, the back bone.'

Ritz

Ritz or *ritzy*, denotes anything that is luxurious, fashionable, and chic. Although the Ritz Hotel itself is nowadays more known, nostalgically, for its opulence than for the wit and style of older days, the sense of panache inherent in the adjective lingers.

The hotelier César Ritz was born in 1850 in Neiderwald, Switzerland, the thirteenth child of a Swiss peasant. In 1866 he became apprentice wine waiter to the main hotel in the town of Brieg. 'You'll never make anything of yourself in the hotel business,' the young Ritz was told by the patron. 'It takes a special knack, a special flair, and it's only right that I should tell you the truth – you haven't got it.'

However, Ritz's career was soon flourishing. He took jobs in hotels across Europe, making friends with the rich and famous, who were later to remember him and patronize his own hotels. In Paris during the siege following the Franco-Prussian War of 1870, Ritz found himself with his friend Escoffier, the master chef, running a restaurant. They raided the Paris Zoo to embellish their meat supplies. Elephant trunk *sauce casseur* became a favourite and elephant blood pudding was reportedly very tasty.

In the 1880s Ritz became manager of London's newly opened Savoy. From there he went on to open the Paris Ritz. But he overworked and in 1902 had a breakdown. Another followed the next year and he ended his days in a clinic near Lucerne. According to his wife he 'gradually sank out of life', and died in 1918.

His own connection with the London Ritz – the hotel he had long dreamed of – was slight. It opened in 1906 and became the gathering place for bright young things, especially in the postwar twenties. Lady Diana Cooper recalls that the Ritz in the thirties was 'the only place where mothers would let young girls go unchaperoned'. Its parties were legendary, and included the memorable occasion when Anna Pavlova emerged from a basket of flowers to dance for guests at a party being held by the American Mrs Gordon.

During the Second World War, the Ritz continued to flourish, both as a social venue (Chips Channon said, 'Ritzes always thrive in wartime, as we are all cookless') and as the meeting place for politicians. In its colourful and long history, the Ritz has seen many aspects of life – from love affairs and terminated engagements to divorce, birth, death and even suicide and murder.

There are Ritz biscuits, a Ritz magazine, Ritz watches, other Ritz hotels. Irving Berlin even wrote a song, sung by Fred Astaire, entitled 'Putting on the Ritz'. As the public relations officer of the Ritz drily observed, 'It's a pity that they didn't patent the name. . . .'

Roscian

The adjective *roscian* denotes eminence in any field of the performing arts. The name derives from the brilliant comic actor of the first century BC, Quintus Roscius. He was born in the Sabine region, became a friend of Cicero and enjoyed the patronage of the famous. He reached such a degree of perfection on the stage that the adjective has been applied ever since to anyone who comes near to reaching his high standards.

Shakespeare credits Roscius's prolific work and versatility, in *Henry VI* Part 3: 'What scene of death hath Roscius now to act?'

Sadism

Sexual pleasure gained through inflicting pain or
humiliation on others or on animals. The Marquis de
Sade's life was no less impressive than the literary legacy he
left behind him, along with the word *sadism*. Donatien
Alphonse de Sade, generally known as the Marquis de Sade,
was born in 1740. His childhood was rich, pampered and
idyllic. Although de Sade was only 5 feet 2 inches tall, he
was handsome. At the age of fourteen he entered the army,
then married Renée-Pelgie de Montreuil, the plain eldest
daughter of the president of the third chamber of the High
Court of Paris, in 1763. She towered over the Marquis in
stature but, although reluctant at first, was so bewitched by
his impeccable pedigree that she hastily agreed to the
match.

From the date of his marriage the life of de Sade began to
deteriorate. Within a few months he was arrested by the
police while in a whorehouse outside Paris. The exact
wording of the charge is now lost but it is fairly certain that
the Marquis was found guilty of sodomy and sentenced to
two months' imprisonment. On his release he retired to his
chateau in Provence.

For several years afterwards he managed his affairs with
reasonable discretion. Then he was arrested again, this
time charged with assault and torture in what came to be
known as the Rose Keller affair. The trial received a great
deal of publicity and de Sade was once again jailed. On his
release he retired again to the country. It was at this point
that his wife's younger sister came to live with them. She
was pretty, witty and gay – everything de Sade's wife was
not – and a relationship sprang up between de Sade and his
sister-in-law. This, not surprisingly, caused problems and
de Sade was forced to flee from police, family and, indeed,
from France altogether. In the end his whereabouts in
Sardinia was discovered and he was brought back to
France. Bar one escape and six short weeks of freedom, de
Sade spent the next thirteen years in jail. While behind
bars, he wrote treatises on Utopia, on politics and on
sociological subjects. He also wrote his famous, ferociously
sensual novels. *The 120 Days of Sodom*, in which he lists 600
variations of the sexual act, took thirty-seven days to

write on a roll of paper 39 feet long. *Justine* (1791) took half the time to write.

During the French Revolution de Sade was transferred to an asylum, only ten days before the storming of the Bastille on July 1789. He was finally released at the age of fifty, fat, rheumatoid and almost penniless.

However, his political activities soon resulted in further spells in jail and it was only due to intense overcrowding and bureaucratic confusion that he escaped with his life. After the Revolution, de Sade eked out his time as a stage manager until Napoleon came to power. De Sade circulated a scurrilous pamphlet containing portraits of Napoleon and Josephine and was once again arrested and this time sent to the lunatic asylum in Charenton, where he spent the last thirteen years of his life. There he acquired a degree of fame for his staging of theatrical productions for the inmates.

De Sade's life taught people, a century before Freud, that there is a lust for cruelty in this world. 'As for my vices – unrestrainable rages – and extreme tendency in everything to lose control of myself, a disordered imagination in sexual matters such as had never been known in this world, an atheist to the point of fanaticism – in two words that I am,' de Sade once wrote. 'And so once again kill me or take me like that, because I shall never change.' He died in 1814.

Saint Vitus's Dance
Saint Vitus's dance is chorea, an illness that affects the central nervous system, causing severe loss of physical control.

Saint Vitus was a young Roman who suffered martyrdom, together with his nurse and his tutor, during the persecutions of the Emperor Diocletian in the early fourth century. Their deaths are annually commemorated on 15 June.

The association of the saint's name with this nervous disease, usually contracted in childhood or early adolescence, dates from the seventeenth century. It was the custom of young people to dance round a statue of Saint Vitus, as it was believed to be a way of ensuring good health. The custom was most prevalent in Germany, where the dancing frequently reached a degree of frenzy. In this way, St Vitus became known as the saint who would protect

people against nervous disorders, hydrophobia and the like
– eventually having one particular illness named after him.

Sam Browne

A brown leather belt with a supporting strap over the right
shoulder originally introduced for wear by British army
officers as a sword belt. A luminous version of the Sam
Browne is worn by police, motorcyclists and pedal-cyclists
to increase their visibility on roads at night.

General Sir Samuel Browne (1824–1901) was born in
India. He was a hero of the Indian Mutiny, during which he
won the Victoria Cross and lost an arm. He rose to the rank
of general in the army and in the 1880s he invented his
sword belt, which is still worn today all over the world.

Sandwich

Next to wellington, *sandwich* is probably the best-known
eponym in the English language. As with many other
eponyms, the bread-and-filling snack had been in existence
long before it received its now common name. But it
took John Montagu, the Fourth Earl of Sandwich
(1718–92), to formalize the idea. Montagu was a
notorious gambler who would often indulge in marathon
card games, refusing to leave his seat in order to eat. During
one session in 1762 he spent twenty-four hours at the table
and commanded his valet to bring him constant supplies of
sliced beef between two pieces of bread; thus the basis of the
picnic lunch was born.

Sandwich was notorious in other ways. He was politically
outspoken and corrupt and, having led the prosecution of a
former friend, was characterized in John Gay's *The Beggar's
Opera* as the loathsome Jemmy Twitcher who impeaches his
friend Macheath – a nickname that followed him thoughout
his life. He was once described as:

> *Too infamous to have a friend,*
> *Too bad for bad men to commend.*
> (Charles Churchill, *The Duellist*, 1763)

Generally a fairly odious character, he apparently looked
the part, someone once describing him as having the
appearance of one who had been half-hanged and cut down
by mistake. He also had a funny shambling walk, such that

seeing him from a distance a colleague remarked, 'I am sure it is Lord Sandwich; for, if you will observe, he is walking from both sides of the street at once.'

He was First Sea Lord when James Cook was sailing the world in search of new lands and conquests, and the Sandwich Islands in the Pacific were named in his 'honour'.

Sandwich died at the age of seventy-four. Two centuries later he is remembered for the innocent and enjoyable sandwich and the blue seas and skies of the Pacific, rather than for the infamy associated with him during his lifetime.

Sanforize

The process of pre-shrinking cotton by mechanical compression of the fibres was invented by Sandford Lockwood Cluett (1874–1968), one of a family of shirt and collar manufacturers in Troy, New York.

Santa Claus

The legendary character who brings children presents at Christmas and who is one of the commercial world's best-loved figures derives his name from Sante Klaas, the Dutch version of St Nicholas.

The cult of St Nicholas was at its height in the Middle Ages; he was without doubt the most popular saint of the time, and no less than 2500 Roman Catholic churches were built in his honour in that period alone. However, who St Nicholas really was is not entirely clear. The main body of opinion seems to be that he was a combination of two separate saints of that name: one the so-called 'boy bishop' of Myra, in what is now Turkey, who died in AD 326. He became a bishop as a very young man and was subsequently adopted as the patron saint of scholars and schoolboys. The other candidate is the sixth-century St Nicholas of Sion. It seems that Nicholas's main claim to saintliness was the miracle he worked in which three generals unjustly condemned by Constantine I to be executed were pardoned after Nicholas had appeared to the Emperor in dreams.

Another story goes that Nicholas miraculously restored to life two children who had been chopped up by a butcher and put in a salting vat! However, perhaps more relevant to his modern occupation is the tale of how he saved three daughters of a poor merchant from being forced by poverty into prostitution by secretly providing dowries for them. Apparently he crept up beneath their bedroom window one night and tossed three bags of gold through the opening, one of which landed in a stocking that had been hung up by the chimney to dry – hence the custom of hanging up stockings for presents.

The cult of St Nicholas is supposed to have been introduced into Germany and Western Europe by the wife of Emperor Otto II in the tenth century. At this period St Nicholas's day was deemed to be 6 December; on the previous evening boys would dress up as bishops and distribute gifts in his honour. The change of date to coincide with other end-of-year celebrations and the appellation Father Christmas came about much later.

Saxophone

The *saxophone*, a brass wind instrument with a clarinet mouthpiece popular with jazz musicians, was invented by Antoine Joseph (known as Adolphe) Sax.

He was born in Dinant, Belgium, in 1814, one of eleven children of Charles Sax, himself a maker of musical instruments. Adolphe trained in his father's business, and from an early age showed unusual aptitude. Having studied flute and clarinet at the Brussels Conservatoire, he went to Paris in 1842 with his saxophone – an attempt to improve the tone of the bass clarinet. He patented the invention in 1846 and, with his father, went on to produce the saxhorn, saxotromba and saxtuba. In 1857 he was appointed instructor in the saxophone at the Paris Conservatoire.

Intended primarily for military bands, the saxophone was quickly adopted by the French army and varieties from alto to baritone are still used today in military bands. Dance bands and 'Big' bands of the 1940s used massed saxophones in their line-ups and Debussy, Glazunov and Ibert have all written music for the instrument. Many world-famous jazz musicians such as Charlie Parker, Colman Hawkins and Lester Young have achieved international eminence playing the saxophone.

Despite the tremendous success of the instrument, Sax

himself received scant reward for his invention and was twice declared bankrupt before dying in poverty in 1894.

Shrapnel
An exploding shell containing bullets.

Lieutenant General Henry Shrapnel was not personally present during the final defeat of Napoleon's forces on 18 June 1815, but his invention was. After the battle, Sir George Wood wrote to Shrapnel to say that the battle would have been lost were it not for his shells, and that it would have been impossible for the British to have recovered the farmhouse of La Haye Sainte without it. 'And hence,' he concluded, 'on this simple circumstance hinged entirely the turn of the battle.'

Henry Shrapnel, one of nine children, was born in Bradford-on-Avon in 1761. He joined the army and received a commission at eighteen, serving as an artillery officer in Gibraltar, the West Indies and Newfoundland. He also proved a great asset to the Duke of York in Flanders when, during a retreat, he saw that the soldiers were having tremendous problems pulling carts across sand. His simple suggestion of locking the wheels so they would slide saved the day.

Invented *c.* 1802, Shrapnel's device was first used in action in Surinam against the Dutch. Originally called 'spherical case-shot', it consisted of a spherical container filled with gunpowder and musket balls. Shrapnel itself has now been largely superseded by other kinds of weapons, but the term is still used by journalists to describe metal splinters from high-explosive shells.

Though promoted to Lieutenant General in 1837, Shrapnel was never adequately recompensed for his invention. He died in 1842.

Shyster
An American slang word meaning one who is professionally unscrupulous. *Shyster* comes from a Mr Scheuster, a successful American criminal lawyer of the 1840s who was often criticized for pettifoggery.

Sideburn (or burnside)

Sideburns, the side whiskers worn by some men, used to be known as burnsides after the Union general Ambrose Everett Burnside.

Burnside (1824–81) was born at Liberty, Indiana. After serving an apprenticeship as a tailor, he went to West Point and later joined the army as a lieutenant in the artillery. He resigned in 1853 to manufacture a breech-loading rifle which he had invented, but the enterprise failed and he entered commerce, eventually becoming treasurer of the Union's Central Railroad. In 1861 he formed and became colonel of the first Rhode Island Regiment and with the outbreak of the American Civil War proved a good soldier, rising to the rank of general. But, it was Burnside who attacked General Lee near Fredericksburg on 13 December 1862 with disastrous consequences. None the less, Burnside survived the Civil War and in 1874 was elected to the US Senate. His gallantry was much admired in Washington social circles, as were his whiskers, thought their name was transposed to *sideburns* by a later less reverent generation.

Silhouette

A *silhouette* is a profile or shadow outline of a face, filled in with a solid, dark colour, generally black. Often these pictures are cut out of thin black paper and the very best examples reveal a high standard of craftsmanship and delicacy.

Silhouettes go back to the Etruscans and beyond, but the term was first used in the eighteenth century. A particularly parsimonious French finance minister, Etienne de Silhouette (1709–67), was made controller general in 1759 through the influence of Madame de Pompadour. He introduced very stringent taxation measures to improve the French economy after the Seven Years' War. These included income tax, a sales tax and even a ruling that unmarried men should pay three times as much as everyone else. This naturally made him very unpopular, and after only four months in office he was forced to resign.

His name came to be associated with anything made 'on the cheap' and *à la Silhouette* became a common phrase – breeches with no pockets even being so described. Whether the portraits that carry his name were so called because they were inexpensive to make or because it was a hobby of the politician himself is not clear. However, the pictures, made originally by tracing the subjects' profile projected onto a piece of paper by the light of a candle, became immensely popular. Goethe was an exponent of the art.

Simony

Today *simony* means traffic in religious and sacred objects with intent to gain. Simon Magus (*fl. c.* AD 37) was a native of Samaria and a reformed wizard, who, on seeing the transformations carried out by St Peter and St John as they conferred the Holy Ghost (Acts 8:18), offered them money if they would give him the gift. Simony, in the form of selling indulgences, etc., was particularly rife in the Middle Ages.

Singer

Singer is possibly the most famous name in sewing machines.

Isaac Merritt Singer (1811–75) was an American inventor and manufacturer. Apart from his sewing machine, he also invented and patented a rock drilling and a carving machine. The single-thread, chain-stitch sewing machine was invented in 1852 and although Singer had to pay another inventor, Elias Howe, for the use of the Howe needles, the fortune and fame of the Singer Company were assured from then on.

Sloane Ranger

Sloane Rangers, the name given to a particular breed of upper-class young ladies and coined by Peter York of *Harper's and Queen* magazine, take their name from Sloane Square and several rather fashionable neighbouring streets in London.

The Sloanes are named after Sir Hans Sloane (his christian name was given to Hans Place), the British physician and collector, who was born in Ireland in 1660. In 1716 he was created a baronet, the first medical practitioner to be so honoured. He became president of the Royal College of Physicians and president of the Royal

Society. His other great interest in life was botany and he founded the Botanical Gardens in 1721; after his death in 1752 his impressive collection of botanical samples and papers were donated to the nation and formed the basis for the collection opened as the British Museum in 1759.

Sloane Square is in the heart of Chelsea, long a favourite area of London for the young, wealthy, well-bred single girl sharing a flat with her old schoolfriends. The similarities in style, manners and dress of these jolly nice girls caught the attention of *Harper's and Queen*, which immortalized their existence in an article entitled 'The Sloane Rangers', published in October 1975. This describes Sloane Rangers as 'the nicest British girls. They wear Gucci not because they want to seem international girls, Eurogirls, but because there's something archaic, pageboyish about them; and Hermès scarves because they, too, are archaic and unmistakable . . . and navy blue because it Always Looks Good.' The serious, worthy Dr Sloane should no doubt be turning in his grave.

Smart Alec(k)

A common term denoting a conceited, bumptious know-all. This description reputedly originated in America in the 1860s and reached the U K some sixty years later, but some sources claim that it was first used in the sixteenth century, after a notable scholar called Alexander Ross who was possessed of such tiresome qualities.

Sole Véronique

This French fish dish, sole prepared with a white wine and grape sauce, was invented by M. Malley, *saucier* at the Ritz, Paris, and later *chef des cuisines* at the Ritz, London.

A special party had been planned and Malley decided to add tiny white grapes to the white wine sauce for the fish course. He gave instructions to a trusted underchef and went out, as was his wont, for the afternoon. When he returned, he found the young man so excited that he could hardly work. M. Malley discovered that the young man's wife had just had a baby girl, their first child. M. Malley asked what they would name their child. 'Véronique,' was the reply. '*Alors,*' said the great chef, 'we'll call the new dish *filet de sole Véronique*'.

Sousaphone

A *sousaphone* is a type of bass tuba much used by marching brass bands. It was invented by John Philip Sousa, the American bandmaster and composer known as 'The March King', who was born in Washington in 1854. His early training as a conductor was with theatre orchestras, but in 1880 he became the conductor of the United States Marine Band. Twelve years later he formed his own band, and soon won international repute with it. Sousa wrote more than 100 popular marches, including 'The Stars and Stripes Forever' (1897) and 'The Washington Post' (1889) and composed ten comic operas, the most successful of which was *El Captain* (1896). He designed the sousaphone in 1899 specifically for marching bands and it quickly established itself amongst bass players and the public alike. Sousa died in 1932.

Spencer

Originally this was a short double-breasted overcoat without skirts worn by men in the late eighteenth and early nineteenth centuries. It was devised by George John Spencer, the Second Earl Spencer (1758–1834), and named after him. He wagered that he could set a new fashion simply by wearing the coat himself, and he won. Spencers became very popular among stylish young men. In the early nineteenth century the same name was also given to a short closely fitting jacket worn by women.

Spinet

A *spinet* is a keyboard instrument common in England in the eighteenth century. It closely resembles the harpsichord, but is slightly smaller and has only one string to each note. The instrument was invented by Giovanni Spinetti, a Venetian musical instrument manufacturer, *c.* 1500. Another derivation for its name is based on the fact that the strings of a spinet are plucked by quills of thorn-like design (Italian *spinetta*, little thorn) rather than being struck by hammers as in the pianoforte.

Spoonerism

A *spoonerism* is the accidental or deliberate transposition of the initial letters of several words, so as to create a bizarre or unconsciously funny combination. The word is derived from Rev. W. A. Spooner (1844–1930) Warden of New College, Oxford, who was well known for his absentmindedness and muddled thinking. He was albino and, as a consequence, suffered from very weak eyesight and nerves; his spoonerisms tended to occur when he was overwrought. Among his best-known phrases are the following:

'We all know what it is to have a half-warmed fish within us.' (half-formed wish)

'Yes, indeed; the Lord is a shoving leopard.'

'Kinquering kongs their titles take.'

Perhaps his most famous blunder occurred when he was in the process of dismissing a student from the college. Blustering with indignation, he turned to the undergraduate and said, 'You have deliberately tasted two worms and you can leave Oxford by the town drain.'

His students were quick to pick up his confusions and invented many fine spoonerisms of their own, such as the (unattributable) story of a don whose bicycle squeaked demanding 'a well-boiled icicle'.

Sometimes the term *spoonerism* is applied to the accidental transposition of whole words, as when the tea-shop waitress was asked for 'a glass bun and a bath of milk'.

Stentorian

A *stentorian* voice is one that is very loud. The adjective originates from Stentor, a Greek herald during the Trojan wars. According to Homer in the *Iliad*, (5: 785): 'There the Goddess, white armed Hera, stood and shouted in the likeness of great hearted Stentor of the brazen voice, whose voice is as the voice of fifty other men.'

A *stentor* is also a variety of microscopic animal shaped like a trumpet.

Stetson

A *stetson* is a high-crowned, wide-brimmed felt hat
traditionally worn by cowboys and frontiersmen in
America. The hats were originally made by John B. Stetson
(1830–1906), who in 1865 founded a one-man
hat-producing company in Philadelphia. The hats were
enormously popular from the outset and Stetson soon had a
turnover of two million hats a year.

'Big hat, no cattle' is a common American expression,
used to describe someone who pretends to be something he
isn't.

Tam-o'-shanter

The name *tam-o'-shanter*, used to describe the round woollen
or cloth cap that fits snugly to the head, close-fitting round
the brow, full above, and with a pompom in the centre, is
taken from the hero of Robert Burns's poem *Tam O'Shanter*
(1789). Often the hat, whose name can be shortened to
tammy, can be seen, in pictures and cartoons, worn by the
poet himself. It was the standard headgear for Scottish
ploughmen.

Burns wrote the poem while walking along the banks of
the river Nith. The character Tam was based on Douglas
Grahame, a local farmer.

Tantalize

To torment by withholding a desired object.

In Greek mythology, Tantalus was a Lydian king who
tested his friendship with the gods to such an extent that
they tired of him and decided to punish him. He was
condemned to everlasting torment in the infernal regions.
His punishment consisted of having to suffer continual
hunger and thirst. Luscious fruit grew just out of his reach
and the waters of Hades always receded when he went to
drink. He was, in short, *tantalized*.

In addition to the verb, Tantalus also left another name
behind him. The *tantalus* is appropriately named. It is a set
of glass decanters locked up in a wooden case. The liquid
contents are visible, but unobtainable without the key.

Tawdry

Any object that is bright and garish, but worthless, may be described as *tawdry*. The word is a corruption of the name Audrey, from St Audrey or Ethelrida. Born in Suffolk, she was the daughter of King Anna of East Anglia and on the death of her first husband retired to the island of Ely, which had been given her as a wedding present. Five years later a marriage was arranged to a boy prince, whom she deserted when he reached manhood. After living for a time in a convent, she set up a monastery on Ely in 672. She died on 23 June 679 of a breast tumour, which she blamed on wearing jewel necklaces as a child. As a result it became fashionable to wear silk necklaces thereafter, which, by comparison, were also much cheaper. At St Audrey's fair, held annually on 23 June, cheap necklaces were a speciality, whether in silk or just 'show' jewellery; hence the origin of the word *tawdry*.

Teddy bears

A stuffed figure of a bear, in plush, used as a toy.

In 1903, in the second year of his presidency, Theodore Roosevelt (1858–1919) went down to Mississippi to hunt bear in the country around Little Sunflower River. His hosts were extremely anxious that the President should make a kill, so they stunned a small brown bear and tied it to a tree. Roosevelt, however, refused to have anything to do with such unsporting behaviour – he was more interested in the hunt than in killing.

The American press heard about the story and Clifford K. Berryman, a cartoonist with the *Washington Post*, produced a cartoon of the scene. The manufacturers of stuffed toy bears, known in those days simply as stuffed bears, pounced on the idea and soon produced the *teddy bear* – and the name has remained.

The joke about the teddy bear followed Roosevelt. In 1911 he went to Cambridge to collect an honorary degree and was met by a double line of students flanking the path. At the end, its paws stretched out in greeting, was a huge teddy bear. Later on in the ceremony, as he was actually receiving his doctorate, a huge teddy bear was lowered down from the roof. Roosevelt discovered, on inquiry, that a similar joke had been played on Darwin when he had gone to Cambridge to receive his honorary degree – but in Darwin's case the animal descending from the rafters was not a bear but a monkey.

Tich

Any small person can be called *tich* (or *titch*). The word derives from the nickname Little Tich, which was given to the music-hall comedian Harry Ralph (1868–1928). When he was a child he was very fat; while he was growing up, the Tichborne case was heard and he was nicknamed Tich in allusion to the Tichborne claimant, who was also corpulent.

The Tichborne case itself was possibly the most celebrated example of impersonation ever to come before the English law courts. In March 1853, Roger Charles Tichborne, heir to an ancient Hampshire baronetcy, set off to travel in South America. On 20 April 1854 he boarded the ship *Bella* bound for Jamaica. The ship went down, all crew and passengers were presumed lost, and for the time being that was the last anyone heard of Charles Tichborne. However, eleven years later, in Wagga Wagga, Australia, a certain R. C. Tichborne turned up. In January 1867 he reached Paris and stepped forward to claim his inheritance. His mother, in her relief at supposedly finding her long-lost son and heir, believed the man to be genuine. The rest of the family, no doubt with their own eyes firmly fixed on their own purses, were not so easily conned. They brought the case to trial, claiming that this R. C. Tichborne was an imposter, and won. The trial lasted for 188 days and the man was identified as Arthur Orton, a butcher from Wapping. He was sentenced to fourteen years' penal servitude. Released in 1884, he later confessed to the imposture in 1895. He died three years later.

Harry Ralph, bearing his celebrated nickname Little Tich, achieved considerable success in his own lifetime. He became renowned for his stage pranks and satirical humour, especially at the Theatre Royal, Drury Lane. His popularity in Paris gained him the Légion d'Honneur.

Titian

The painter Titian was a great master of colour and the adjective *titian* is used today to describe particularly lustrous red hair of a bright golden auburn hue, often featured in his portraits. Tiziano Vecelli was born at Pieve di Cadore in the Friulian Alps. There is controversy surrounding the year of his birth: Titian himself indicated that he was born in 1477 but from available documentation the year 1490 seems more likely. He studied under the great masters Bellini and Giorgione and their influence can be seen in his early painting. The first works that are solely attributable to him – and which demonstrate his unique style – are three frescoes of scenes of the life of Saint Anthony at Padua (1511).

Titian is seen as being the finest exponent of the Venetian School of painters. He was appointed official painter to the council in Venice in 1516 and was made Count Palatine and Knight of the Golden Spur by Emperor Charles V. He died of the plague in 1576.

Tom Collins

Tom Collins cocktails are versions of gin slings – of which the Singapore sling is perhaps the most famous. Basically a Tom Collins is any drink which roughly resembles the original mixture of gin, lemon or lime juice, sugar and soda water. It was named after a nineteenth-century bartender, Tom Collins, who worked at Limmer's Old House in London.

Tontine

A *tontine* is a form of annuity shared by several subscribers. The arrangement is that whenever a member of the group dies, his share is added to those of the surviving members. The one who survives the longest enjoys the whole income.

This system was named after a Neapolitan banker, Lorenzo Tonti, who introduced the idea into French financial circles in 1653. It was first put into effect in 1689 by Louis XIV, who attracted no less than 1,400,000 subscriptions. When the last survivor died thirty-seven years later she was drawing a 2300 per cent larger dividend than her original investment. In 1765, the House of

Commons raised £300,000 by way of tontine annuities
at 3 per cent. A notable example of the use of the system
took place in 1871, when the *Daily News* proposed tontine to
raise £650,000 to purchase the Alexandra Palace and 100
acres of land.

Trilby

The soft felt hat with an indented crown, universally called
a *trilby*, took its name from the heroine of George du
Maurier's novel *Trilby*, published in 1894. The hats were
worn in the original London stage production based on the
novel (1895).

The novel is the story of Trilby O'Ferrall, an artist's
model living in Paris, with whom several young students
fall madly in love. She herself falls under the influence of
Svengali, a German–Polish musician, who hypnotizes her.
Under his power, she becomes a famous singer. However,
her fame and prowess are so dependent on him that when he
dies she loses her voice, languishes and eventually dies.

Du Maurier was born and educated in Paris, though his
mother was English. His novel also added another word to
the language – *Svengali*, used to denote a person with great
hypnotic and forceful powers.

Du Maurier, who died in 1896, was the father of the actor
Sir Gerald du Maurier and the grandfather of the author
Daphne du Maurier.

Trudgen

The *trudgen* swimming stroke, which involves a double
overarm breast stroke motion and a scissors kick, was
introduced into Britain by John Trudgen, an English
swimmer who lived from 1852 to 1902. He apparently
learned the stroke from the Argentinians while he was
staying in Buenos Aires in 1863.

Tureen

A huge serving bowl with a lid, specifically for soup.

The Vicomte de Turenne (1611–75) was one of the
greatest figures of seventeenth-century French military
history and was created Marshal General of France in 1660.
On one occasion there were no bowls available in which to

serve the soup; he whipped off his helmet, upturned it, poured in the soup and thereby founded a dynasty of dinner dishes.

One of history's more famous tureens is a Meissen tureen which can be seen in Blenheim Palace. The handles are in the shape of lemon slices. It is part of a large service presented by the King of Poland to the Fourth Duke of Marlborough; the King's return gift was a pack of staghounds.

Another derivation of the word is from terrine, an earthenware dish (Latin *terra*, earth).

Uncle Tom

The book *Uncle Tom's Cabin* by Harriet Beecher Stowe (1811–96), published in 1852, features a cheerfully subservient Negro, Uncle Tom. The story tells of the sale of a pious, faithful old Negro slave to a bad owner. In its time it drew attention to the plight of the Negroes and helped to rouse America to an understanding of the iniquities of the slave system. Beecher Stowe based her novel on fact; her Uncle Tom was a slave who was subsequently ordained, becoming the Reverend Josiah Henson.

Henson (1789–1883) was born into slavery on a Maryland farm. He became the overseer of his master's estate and a Methodist lay preacher. On learning that he was to be sold to a Southern planter, he escaped from Maryland to Canada, taking his wife and large family with him. He visited England on three occasions, calling for the emancipation of slaves, and in 1876 was presented to Queen Victoria.

Nowadays the term *Uncle Tom* is used derisively among Black people to describe any Negro who is thought to be subservient to the White establishment.

Valentine

Valentine cards, containing endearments and usually anonymous, are sent to loved ones on 14 February each year.

There were two St Valentines in history and both became

martyrs for their Christian belief. The first was a priest of
Rome who was imprisoned for succouring persecuted
Christians. He is supposed to have restored the sight of the
jailer's blind daughter. He was clubbed to death *c*. 270 BC.
The other St Valentine, Bishop of Terni, was martyred for
his beliefs a few years later.

The association of these two siants with romance has
more to do with the date of their death than the manner of
their life or martyrdom. In the Middle Ages 14 February
was associated with the beginning of spring and the mating
of birds; as a result the saints' name was given to human
courting cards sent on this day. In *A Midsummer Night's
Dream*, Shakespeare wrote:

> *Good morrow, friends! St Valentine is past;*
> *Begin these wood-birds but to couple now?*

Valentines were immensely popular in Victorian times
and in recent years the industry has thrived.

The day of St Valentine is also connected with the
Roman festival of Lupercalia (15 February).

Van Dyck

The Flemish painter who lived during the reign of Charles I
left his name to two English words. The most noted
describes the small trim pointed beard sported not only by
Van Dyck himself, but also by many of the famous people
who posed for him. Charles I himself was one of these.

His other eponym refers to the scalloped collars of shirts
and jackets that most of the subjects of his portraits wore, a
fashion subsequently adopted by women only.

Sir Anthony Van Dyck was born in Antwerp in 1599, the
seventh of twelve children of a silk merchant. He became a
pupil of Rubens. When he was twenty-one he came to
England in the employment of King James I; after a brief
stay, Van Dyck travelled round Europe and settled in
Antwerp. He finally returned to England in 1632 to become
'principalle Paynter in ordinary of their Majesties' to
Charles I, receiving a gold chain and a salary of £200 per
annum. He was knighted and installed in a house in
Blackfriars, with a country residence at Eltham Palace. His
marriage to a Scotswoman, Lady Mary Ruthven, was also
personally arranged by the king.

Van Dyck was a business-like painter, never allowing more than an hour at a time to a sitter. He was also a frustrated man, who, although a brilliant portrait painter, would have preferred to have worked on historical subjects. He died in 1641 and was buried at Old St Pauls.

Volt

The *volt*, the primary unit of measure of electromotive force, was defined and named by the Italian physicist Count Allessandro Volta (1745–1827).

Volta was born in Como, Italy, and became professor of natural philosophy at Pavia. While there he developed the theory of constant current electricity, a volt being defined as the difference of potential capable of sending a current of 1 amp through a conductor whose resistance is 1 ohm. He also invented the first battery, known as the voltaic pile, the hydrogen lamp (1777) and the electrophorus. He was summoned to show his discoveries to Napoleon (1801) and received medals and awards both at home and abroad, including the Royal Society's Copley Medal, which he received in 1794. He retired in 1819 and died eight years later.

Watt

In the 1880s the *watt* was officially adopted as the standard unit of electrical power. More precisely, a watt is the rate of work represented by a current of 1 amp under a pressure of 1 volt.

James Watt (1736–1819) was born at Greenock, in Scotland, the son of a mathematical instrument-maker. After studying at Glasgow University and spending a year in London, he set up business in Glasgow but encountered difficulties. Then Glasgow University employed him as its official instrument-maker and, among other things, he helped with surveys for the Forth and Clyde Canal.

He had long been interested in steam power. In 1764 a working model of the Newcomen pumping engine had been sent to him for repair. Not only did he repair it but he removed a large number of defects which he noticed in the machine. He introduced an air pump, a steam-jacket for the

cylinder, and added a separate condenser. All these
modifications he patented in 1769. Then, with Matthew
Boulton, an engineer from Birmingham, he entered into
partnership to manufacture new engines.

Watt's machines soon excelled anything available, and
he also obtained patents for numerous other inventions;
including the sun-and-planet gear-wheel mechanism, the
expansion principle, the double-action engine and the
parallel-motion link. He also invented a letter-copying
press, a screw propeller and a machine for reproducing
scuplture. The term *horsepower* was originated by Watt and
Boulton, a watt being $1/746$th hp.

Wedgwood

Josiah Wedgwood left his name in three ways: first, his
pottery and its particular style; second, the hazy blue colour
which is the distinctive hallmark of Wedgwood china; and,
third, as a term to designate the temperature scale used in
the pyrometer invented by Wedgwood for testing the heat of
a kiln.

He was born in 1730 at Burslem, Staffordshire. His
family had long been involved in pottery-making, but in
those days English pottery was of little account and most
ordinary china came from Delft, in Holland, while finer
porcelains were imported direct from China.

Wedgwood had no education, except for learning his
family trade. As a child he was severely ill and had to have
his right leg amputated; this disability debarred him from
using the potter's wheel. He began instead to make modest
experiments with clays, firing and design that were later to
revolutionize English pottery standards. He designed and
manufactured tableware and, later, a white stoneware that
attracted the attention of the rich, the famous and the royal,
in particular Queen Charlotte.

His business boomed, particularly when he discovered
the genius of John Flaxman as a decorator and designer. He
contributed largely towards the building of the
Trent–Mersey canal and built the village of Etruria, an
early example of an industrial housing estate. Josiah
Wedgwood died in 1795.

Welch

There is dispute about the origin of this expression, which means to renege on a deal, to let someone down, or generally to betray someone. The word was originally only applied to racecourse bookmakers who disappeared instead of paying out. The English like to think that the term *to welch* (or *welsh*) derives from the rhyme 'Taffy was a Welshman, Taffy was a thief, Taffy came to my house and stole a leg of beef'. However, the Welsh take the view that the term originated with a Bob Welch of Epsom, an English bookie who made off with the bets.

Wellington boot

Originally a high leather boot covering the knee in front and cut away behind. Nowadays the word refers to a waterproof rubber boot reaching to the knee. *Wellington* is one of the best-known eponyms in the English language. The boots were named after Arthur Wellesley, the First Duke of Wellington (1769–1852), and one of Britain's finest generals, known as the Iron Duke.

Wellington boots were worn extensively in the army and by the fashionable. 'No gentleman could wear anything in the daytime but wellington boots,' said a contemporary chronicler. Wellington himself sported the boots during both his military and political career, the latter culminating in 1823 when he was asked by King George IV to form a government. He remained Prime Minister until 1830 when he resigned, to be succeeded by Earl Grey. He returned to politics as Foreign Secretary under Peel (1834–36) and as Minister Without Portfolio (1841–46).

Today rubber *wellies* are found in most homes. They were, however, not the only item to which his name was put. The giant fir, the *wellingtonia*, was introduced to Britain from California in 1853 and named after the Duke as a compliment to his political and military achievements. And in the Second World War, one of the RAF's most successful bomber planes was named after him. This eponym developed a sub-eponym, as wellingtons were nicknamed wimpys from a character called J. Wellington Wimpy.

Wisteria (or wistaria)

A pale climbing shrub of the pea family with blue flowers,
native to China, Japan and the USA.

Dr Casper Wistar (1761–1818) was a Philadelphia
Quaker. He was a professor of chemistry and physiology at
the Univeristy of Philadelphia and he wrote the first
American textbook on anatomy. He also succeeded
Thomas Jefferson as president of the American
Philosophical Association from 1815 to 1818. He had his
lighter side too and was famous in Philadelphia for his
Sunday afternoon at-homes. The plant was named in
Wistar's honour at his death in 1818 by Thomas Nuttall.

Yapp

To yapp a book is to protect its edges with leather covers that
droop over the edge of the pages. The process was devised
by a London bookseller called William Yapp, who
specialized in selling evangelical literature. He was a zealot
and always carried a bible in his pocket. Infuriated by its
increasing tattiness, he had his first book yapped and by so
doing bought himself immortality in the pages of larger
dictionaries. Some bibles and prayerbooks are still
produced with yapped bindings.

Yarborough

A *yarborough* is a bad hand in bridge. The term originally
meant any hand of thirteen cards containing no cards
higher in value than nine, although it is sometimes used to
describe a hand which contains no trumps. The name
comes from the Second Earl of Yarborough, an excessively
keen whist-player, who layed odds of 1000 to 1 against any
of his guests ever picking up such a hand. The actual
mathematical odds are 1827 to 1 against, so Lord
Yarborough was on to a fairly safe bet. Although he lived
from 1809 until 1862, it was not until 1900, according to the
Oxford English Dictionary, that the word became an accepted
part of the English language.

The Yarborough home, Brocklesby Park in Lincolnshire,
is said to have been the original for Bleak House.

The opposite to a yarborough, a hand full of kings and

queens, is sometimes known as a *fairbanks*. The allusion is to
Douglas Fairbanks Jr, who took delight in being in the
company of royalty, even if they were only faces on playing
cards.

Yokel

An ignorant peasant. This word apparently derives from
the biblical name Jacob, which in Bohemia was spelt Jokel
(pronounced yokel). Jacob was a common christian name
in the area and the word has come to mean any peasant.
There is also a dialect word *yokel*, meaning green
woodpecker or yellowhammer.

Zany

Zany means *imaginatively comical* or, as a noun, *clown* or
buffoon, but it is also used nowadays to describe anything
offbeat. The word from which it derives, zanni, a corruption
of Giovanni (John) is the name given to the comic servant in
the Italian *commedia dell'arte*. Drawn from the lower class,
these lively tricksters provide most of the humour in the
comedy and usually number amongst their group
Arlecchino (Harlequin), Pulcinella (Punch), Pedrolino
(Pierrot), Mezzotino and Brighella.

Zeppelin
A dirigible airship.

   Count Ferdinand von Zeppelin was born in 1838 on a
small island in Lake Constance, which was then part of the
kingdom of Württemberg. Like most young men of his day,
he joined the army in his late teens and received a
commission in 1859, later joining the Engineer Corps.
Under the pretext of studying army organization, he set sail
for America when the Civil War broke out. He was bound
for the Union army, carrying in one pocket a letter to
President Lincoln and in the other, in the event of capture, a
letter to Robert E. Lee, the commander of the Confederate
armies. While in the States he made his first balloon ascent,
at St Paul, Minnesota. In America he first conceived the
idea of the dirigible – a structure that could be filled with

gas like a balloon but once in the air could be navigated like a ship.

After the Franco-Prussian War of 1870, he began in earnest to draft plans for his airships, plans he kept secret for many years; it was not until he was retired in 1891, having reached the rank of general, that he was able to concentrate on the project. He soon discovered that the airship itself was the least of his problems. German government experts considered the dirigible, *Luftschiff*, *Zeppelin 1*, hopelessly impractical. *LZ.1* made its first flight in the summer of 1900 over Lake Constance. The airship travelled about three and a half miles and landed safely after seventeen minutes in the air; people were delighted, but the government was not convinced. Two more flights followed but were of limited duration and eventually the ageing count sold the dirigible for scrap. News of the sale brought many messages of sympathy and eventually the King of Württemberg set up a state lottery which netted 124,000 DM for the zeppelin.

LZ.4 accomplished a twelve-hour flight at a speed of 40 m.p.h. Zeppelin himself became a national hero and his seventieth birthday was widely celebrated. Despite the disaster that overtook *LZ.4* – it was destroyed by flames during an electrical storm – the general feeling was that a whole fleet of airships should be built.

Count Zeppelin was seventy-six when the First World War began, and he died before the German defeat was final. During the war eighty-eight airships were built and used successfully on bombing raids, the first being over Great Yarmouth in 1915. After the war the *Graf Zeppelin* set a new record by circumnavigating the globe in twenty-one days and until the tragedy of the *Hindenberg* at Lakehurst, USA, in 1937 more than 32,000 people had flown in Zeppelin airships.

Zinnia

An annual flower of the aster family common to the Americas.

Johann Gottfried Zinn (1727–59) was a German botanist who died young, aged thirty-two, but was by that time